Whiteboard Selling

Empowering Sales through Visuals

Whiteboard Selling

Corey Sommers • David Jenkins

WILEY

Published by John Wiley & Sons, Inc., Hoboken, New Jersey.
Published simultaneously in Canada.

For general information about our other products and services, please contact our Customer Care Department within the United States at (800) 762-2974, outside the United States at (317) 572-3993 or fax (317) 572-4002.

Wiley publishes in a variety of print and electronic formats and by print-on-demand. Some material included with standard print versions of this book may not be included in e-books or in print-on-demand. If this book refers to media such as a CD or DVD that is not included in the version you purchased, you may download this material at http://booksupport.wiley.com. For more information about Wiley products, visit www.wiley.com.

Library of Congress Cataloging-in-Publication Data:
Sommers, Corey.
  Whiteboard Selling: Empowering Sales through Visuals/Corey Sommers and David Jenkins.
ISBN: 978-1-118-37976-9 (pbk); ISBN: 978-1-118-61227-9 (ebk); ISBN: 978-1-118-46157-0 (ebk); ISBN: 978-1-118-46155-6 (ebk)
1. Selling–Audio-visual aids. I. Jenkins, David. II. Title.
  HF5438.25
  658.85028′4–dc23
                                                                2013000324

Printed in the United States of America

10 9 8 7 6 5 4 3 2 1

Contents

Foreword

Of all of our inventions for mass communication, pictures still speak the most universally understood language.

—Walt Disney

Knowledge is power. Prior to the early 1990s, salespeople had it—buyers didn't. Today the tables have turned and buyers can now get information about your products and services whenever they need it, thanks to the Internet.

Allow me to expand on this. A commonly held belief among many executive leadership teams is that the keys to a good sales force are: (1) to make sure they have deep product knowledge and (2) that they can deliver a compelling pitch about their products and services. Operating on those beliefs, sales organizations developed deeply ingrained cultures where product training was mandated, centrally prepared and tightly controlled sales decks were developed, and specific step-by-step sales processes were implemented. There was a great deal of focus on the delivery of the sales pitch, and a bevy of feature- and function-rich materials provided as leave-behinds. These methods were effective during most of the twentieth century because salespeople were the most common source of information for buyers. It just made sense to create a business process at the heart of which was control of the information flow to buyers through sellers.

Unfortunately, the preferences of buyers (particularly executive ones) have changed. Due in large part to the Internet, the pendulum has shifted and buyers are often more informed about the products and services than the salespeople. Salespeople who don't add value only add cost to the value exchange. In order to squeeze out costs, professional procurement organizations are increasingly active in more buying negotiations. Since the tables have turned, and these buyers now have more information than their sales counterparts, they are winning. This development is the single biggest driver behind the margin erosion felt by most B2B businesses.

In response, many sales leaders are directing their teams to bypass procurement functions and sell higher in those organizations. The higher the level of executive targeted, the less interested they are in learning about products and services and the more interested they are in the role sellers play in helping them meet objectives or solve problems. Understandably, then, a new form of communication is required but few sales forces have figured out the right formula to elevate who they sell to or how to cross-sell their products. Forrester Research has been studying the perceptions executives have about sellers in our annual buyers insight study. Less than 20 percent of these executives find that the common salesperson adds value, and 68 percent believe salespeople are only wired to launch into some prepared pitch about their products or services. Clearly, something needs to change.

So, why is communicating with executives so different? For starters, the scope of their responsibilities is much broader than their subordinates', so the issues they want to tackle are more holistic in nature. In order to get their arms around all of the moving parts, executives like to visualize the system in order to make sure they have visibility into all of the cause-and-effect relationships they need to address in order to be successful. In addition, these people have risen through the ranks to become leaders in their organizations because they have proven they can produce results. Thus, they are much more inclined to discuss an example about how other customers have worked with your firm to solve problems or meet goals, and they really want to hear about common pitfalls and how other people like them have worked around them. The scope of these conversations and their dynamic nature are not a fit with a traditional product-centric, prepared pitch-driven communication style. It requires a fundamentally different approach.

This is why this book is so important. While the concept of using a whiteboard to communicate complex ideas is not a new one, creating an overall architecture and process for developing the content and equipping salespeople with the skills to create one is. What Corey Sommers and David Jenkins do in this book is to first establish the basic attributes of how a whiteboard discussion framework should be constructed to effectively empower sellers with a safety net to stay relevant to an executive audience, and then show the steps for how to convert prose-based messages into a visual format. Finally, Corey and David provide the common requirements and whiteboarding best practices to properly train salespeople to be effective in client situations. When successfully executed, this new medium of communication allows for much faster ramp-up times of salespeople to deliver a complex message, while at the same time reducing the noise inherent in traditional presentation approaches.

—**Scott Santucci**

Research Director and Principal Analyst
Sales Enablement at Forrester Research

Introduction

Are you a sales professional looking for a new and creative way to engage your enterprise prospects?

Or a marketer determined that sales will use the right messages to attract economic buyers into your sales funnel with a unique and fresh approach?

Or a sales leader, focused on sales transformation, larger transactions, and shorter time-to-close?

If so, then this book is for you.

What if you could sell with nothing more than a pen and a drawing surface? When sales professionals lose the PowerPoint and use the pen, they are more confident, and they are much more likely to compel buyers to act. This book shows you how to make this transformation for yourself or your entire sales and marketing organizations.

We should make it clear up front that although this book is titled *Whiteboard Selling*, this by no means implies we are inventing whiteboarding for sales. Seasoned sales professionals and other customer-facing personnel have been whiteboarding for decades. All we have done is put a heavy dose of structure and process behind building powerful visual stories and discussion frameworks, and then enabling sellers to present them in a way that captivates and motivates buyers.

Is Selling with Visuals a New Idea?

Yes and no. There are literally thousands of books on the power of visual communications, visual thinking, and presentation skills—and not just books, but reams of academic papers, studies, and surveys. Indeed, it is well established that visual thinking, learning, and communication styles and approaches have clear advantages when conducting business. Ours is an increasingly visual culture; we consume media and information through an ever-growing variety of visual channels.

Likewise, there are many books and other publications that detail different sales methodologies and processes. Ask any experienced sales executive and they will recall at least two or three different packaged sales approaches they have been trained on, each with its own twist on convincing corporate buyers to part with their valuable budgets.

How many books have been written on how to build and deliver better PowerPoint presentations? Presenting a set of slides to a customer is not selling with visuals. Selling is a dynamic exercise. Selling should encourage interaction with, and participation from, the buyer. If the buyer is passively observing a set of slides, then you are not using true visual selling.

NOT SELLING WITH VISUALS

How This Book Is Different

So how is this book any different from those mentioned earlier?

It is entirely focused on the power of hands-on visual selling techniques to enable your sales force to sell bigger deals faster. And not just large sales forces—even a small business owner or a few salespeople working at a start-up can use these techniques. If you are going to learn to use visual thinking and communication when you sell, then you have to learn a unique viewpoint and a set of best practices, all of which are contained in this book.

The visual selling techniques and approaches in this book are appropriate to any sales methodology. Enabling sales through visuals can be part of any approach to selling and any sales enablement program. The use of powerful visuals at the point of sale—that moment of truth, so to speak, when a seller is communicating the unique value proposition of their product or service—is just one part (perhaps one of the most important parts) of any larger sales model or sales transformation initiative.

This book contains hands-on, step-by-step guidance on how to design powerful visuals to support your sales process. It is explicitly designed to be a complete and exhaustive companion to any sales and marketing organization's efforts to bring visual selling techniques to its go-to-market strategies. This book is as heavy on practice as it is on theory.

The book is valuable to both sellers and marketers alike. It provides this practical guidance in a way that both sales professionals and marketers can use to become more effective. While the term "bridging the sales and marketing divide" is often overused, in this case it really fits. This book will help get marketing's message out to sales in a usable and powerful fashion.

And finally, this book is based on proven best practices and results demonstrated over half a decade of rigorous application in professional sales environments. More than 50,000 sales professionals in more than 20 countries and belonging to more than 75 sales organizations have benefited from these approaches to dramatically change the way they communicate with customers and prospects.

Is It the Whiteboard That Matters?

Some would argue that drawing on a whiteboard—"whiteboarding"—is not the point and it is really visual thinking and idea creation that matters. This is partly true. But in *Whiteboard Selling—Empowering Sales Through Visuals*, we specifically explore the use of the whiteboard (or any drawing surface for that matter) as a disciplined, repeatable, and process-driven mechanism that enables high-dollar sales of complex products and services targeted at educated buyers.

Using a pen to draw ideas is only useful if it drives a compelling event such as the purchase of a million-dollar software suite, medical device, financial service offering, or consulting service (among many other types of products and services). When you use a drawing surface to sell solutions, you have to understand the sales process and field training/enablement. You have to assess each individual salesperson's proficiency using visual thinking to move a sales opportunity to the next level. Sketching stick figures, smiley faces, and other "cave art" won't increase sales in a meaningful way without understanding the sales context in which they are drawn.

By the end of this book, you'll learn how to train and enable your entire distribution channel with powerful tools and techniques to make the power of the pen a groundbreaking differentiator in how you bring your products and services to market.

How You Should Use This Book

Part 1—The End of the Age of Slides

We've been helping businesses, large, medium, and small, to ditch their slide projectors since 2007. As time goes by, we have to convince our customers and prospects less and less that whiteboard selling has clear advantages over slides for important sales interactions. In the first section of this book, you will learn why slides should play very little role in high-dollar sales interactions and sales training, as demonstrated by real-life stories from the field.

Part 2—The Visual Selling Opportunity

Once you understand that salespeople and sales trainers can actually completely free themselves from the evil clutches of slides and projectors, Part 2 will teach you about the specific opportunities and benefits of leveraging visual selling techniques and the science behind why this is so effective. We'll also highlight some results that may impress.

Part 3—What Exactly Is a Whiteboard for Sales?

In this section we showcase a number of different whiteboard types using a case study to demonstrate whiteboard structure, content, and flow. Part 3 also includes a variety of exercises and activities to flex your whiteboarding muscles.

Part 4—Building a Whiteboard for Sales

Whether you are an individual contributor or the head of a marketing or sales team, you'll need to marshal some key resources—both people and content—before embarking on whiteboard design. Then, we'll show you how to follow some basic and proven whiteboard creation best practices.

Part 5—Enabling the Field

You've designed some powerful whiteboard stories. So what's next? This section covers sales enablement options, how to test-drive your whiteboard prior to field rollout, and then how to measure the success of your whiteboard-selling training initiatives.

Part 6—You Have a Whiteboard, So How Do You Present It and What Do You Leave Behind?

This section covers some basic whiteboard presentation best practices, and how to use the whiteboard as a powerful tool for documenting and communicating the next steps in the sales process.

PART 1

The End of the Age of Slides

CHAPTER 1

The Role of Presentation Slides in Today's Sales Culture

The best way to paralyze an opposition army is to ship it PowerPoint and thereby contaminate its decision making.

—Robert Gaskins, co-creator of PowerPoint

The term "death by PowerPoint" is so prevalent that it is now firmly entrenched in corporate culture. In fact, as of this writing, if you Google this term and look at the Google Images search results, you will see 50,000 images (many of them great comic relief) related to the term. The phrase was actually first coined by Angela Garber in 2001.[1] It was a good article. But like thousands of other articles and books on how to continue to use PowerPoint while avoiding its pitfalls, Garber's piece was just that—suggestions on how to put lipstick on a pig. We ask, "Why not just fry up some bacon?"

So we know that slides are the predominant way organizations communicate internally and between buyers and sellers. But there is now data that shows there are significant, quantifiable costs associated with their use. Right around the twentieth anniversary of PowerPoint, a study cited in the *Wall Street Journal* conservatively estimated $252 million in lost productivity *per day* due to bad slide presentations.[2] The calculation is based on Microsoft's 2001 estimate of 30,000,000 slide presentations in existence. That's in 2001, during PowerPoint's infancy or, at best, its adolescence. How many hundreds of millions of presentations could be out there now? Today's daily PowerPoint productivity drain could be measured in the tens of billions of dollars!

How Did We Get Here?

Something momentous happened in the mid-1980s. Yes, it was the advent of the personal business computer, which was first manufactured by IBM. But more important than that, slide presentation software

---

[1]Angela R. Garber, "Death By PowerPoint," April 1, 2001, www.SmallBusinessComputing.com.

[2]Jared Sandberg, "Tips for PowerPoint: Go Easy on the Text—Please, Spare Us," *Wall Street Journal*, November 14, 2006.

was invented. Word processing, spreadsheet, and slide presentation software promised businesses of the 1980s an immense increase in productivity. They have no doubt reshaped corporate communications. Whether they increase productivity and effectiveness of high-dollar salespeople in the twenty-first century is debatable.

From Foils to Slides

Before slide presentation software existed, the notion of using a foil to communicate a singular idea within a larger presentation was not new. During the two decades prior to the 1980s, we first had the overhead projector with transparencies and then the slide projector, both of which were ubiquitous in college classrooms, government agencies, and corporate meeting rooms. The "pop" of an overhead's worn-out light bulb and the audible "thwack, thwack, thwack" of the stuck projector slide are to some people fond (and to others not so fond) sounds of a bygone era.

When electronic slides arrived—which are, strictly speaking, computer-generated images that include text, graphics, and charts in one program—they were a powerful change in communication. Now the presenter could seamlessly move forward or backward between slides, insert multimedia elements, and integrate with other software programs. The widespread addiction to slideware quickly took hold.

Have We Moved Forward or Backward?

This era of electronic slides created a new communication superpower: PowerPoint. Microsoft PowerPoint quickly became the dominant player in the computer-generated slide market, displacing Harvard Graphics in the late 1980s and early 1990s. Harvard Graphics never gained much traction when the market shifted to Microsoft Windows from DOS, where it had owned almost 70 percent of the market. PowerPoint, with its form and flash, quickly became the software of choice for corporate use, education, and increasingly, in the home.

Since then, PowerPoint has been widely (or should we say "wildly") adopted as *the* way to execute a sales presentation in the corporate office or meeting room. While bad sales presentations have been around almost as long as the sales profession, PowerPoint amplifies bad habits by eliminating the need to think on your feet, study your message, and prepare it diligently. "They tried adding elements from multimedia shows (such as sound effects, attention-grabbing transitions between slides, moving text, and bullet points that flew to their places from somewhere off screen)," says Gaskins. "Much of this was novel and interesting the first few times, but virtually none of the extraneous entertainment had any purpose or benefit in the kinds of meetings where overheads had been used."[3] Not only do these flashy features serve little purpose, they are so overused and badly used that sales presentations become a distraction and even an obstacle to the core purpose of any meeting.

This massive and lightning-fast adoption of the electronic slide has been a step backwards in how sellers communicate the business value of their products and solutions to corporate decision makers. In fact, it can be argued that the move from overhead projector and transparencies to a slide projector was itself regressive. What was gained in form, factor, and flashy visuals was lost in the free form of hand drawing with a grease pen that is actually more like whiteboarding than any technology-based mechanism.

How Slides Harm the Sales Process

While we agree there is a role for slides inside an organization, they become a disaster for big sales opportunities. Having a salesperson plug in a projector and go through an hour-long slide presentation during a first sales meeting doesn't inspire a buyer's confidence. In fact, it could actually damage the salesperson's ability to properly interact

---

[3]Robert Gaskins, 2007, www.robertgaskins.com.

with the client and communicate the business value of a product or solution. Using a slideshow ultimately jeopardizes a sales professional's credibility.

Overwhelming with Slide Candy

With PowerPoint's ever-increasing feature set for animations and other flying eye candy, slide presentations of all types more and more resemble TV commercials. Watching a car commercial is one thing. Feeling sold to in the context of the sale of a product or service that can make or break somebody's job is another.

Many of these problems were echoed by those surveyed by Power-Point expert David Paradi in 2011.[4] Of 603 respondents, the following reasons were given for why slide presentations are not well received:

The speaker read the slides to us	73.8%
Full sentences instead of bullet points	51.6%
The text was so small I couldn't read it	48.1%
Slides hard to see because of color choice	34.0%
Overly complex diagrams or charts	26.0%

Longer Sales Cycles

Is it possible that the use of PowerPoint can elongate sales cycles? Unequivocally, yes! When people are annoyed or distracted from your core message, they won't decide to buy.

Slides invite marketers and sellers alike to pack in product details, features, functions, schematics, architectures, and other "stuff." The format encourages leading with products and features during the first critical sales interactions, when you should be leading with qualification, discovery, and an account of how your solutions can deliver unique business value. With all the attention on products and features, presales and other technical resources are required earlier in the sales cycle, which, in turn, has unfortunate consequences:

- Added cost of sale by requiring technical resources and other subject matter experts (SMEs) on all sales calls, even calls that may not be qualified

---

[4]David Paradi, 2011, www.thinkoutsidetheslide.com.

- Delays due to scheduling conflicts with other people involved
- Unavailability of scarce SMEs for other, better-qualified opportunities

And if a company's solutions aren't appropriately differentiated using slides, sales cycles can drag on with lengthy technical evaluations and proof of concepts.

Slides Get Around

Organizations should also remember that slide presentations are so portable that "PowerPoint sprawl" can deliver your sales approach directly into the hands of your competition. While it may contaminate your competition's thinking, as Gaskins says, the more likely scenario is a loss of competitive advantage. The most common ways a company's PowerPoint and Adobe Acrobat presentations end up on the public Internet are, first, that salespeople give them to customers and partners who post them on publicly accessible websites; or that company workers post them to unprotected parts of their company's *own* websites. Search engines like Google don't really care whether your documents are intended for corporate use or not—they'll sniff them out if there are no safeguards in place.

Try the following Google searches to find out what type of potentially sensitive files are out there on the public Internet:

[your company name] filetype:ppt
[your company name] filetype:pdf
[your company name] filetype:doc
[your company name] filetype:xls
For larger organizations try:
[your company name] "sales presentation" filetype:ppt (pdf)
[your company name] "marketing plan" filetype:ppt (pdf, doc, xls)
[your company name] "sales strategy" filetype:ppt (pdf, doc)

Or try a variety of other keyword combinations. You may be surprised by what you can find out on the Internet.

The Premeeting Slide Shuffle

You know that slides are inflexible, at times annoying and difficult to view, and potentially damaging to your brand and confidential information. So sometimes you decide to customize your slide presentation. Customizations bring their own problems. What will happen when you customize slides at the last minute prior to a presentation that you will be giving to an important buyer? Let's look at a couple of different scenarios.

The Night-Before Change

Let's say you're preparing for a presentation with a mid-level manager the next day using a 30-slide deck. You get a call from your contact that their boss will be in attendance. You can merge in slides from another slide presentation, but that takes you two hours you were planning to spend updating your sales forecast.

The Five-Minutes-Before Change

You learn that the CEO is going to be joining the meeting. You can scramble to hide or reorient slides, but adding new ones from other slide presentations won't be an option. You'll appear to be unorganized and poorly prepared.

The On-the-Fly Change

The attendees in the meeting want to go in a different direction. You could open up a new slide presentation on-screen (and potentially share your client list folder structure!), skip slides, or breeze through slides.

The worst-case scenario is when you lack slides for the topics of most interest to your buyer, or unexpected decision makers or influencers join the meeting and you are not able to incorporate their needs in the presentation. There may be a whiteboard in the room. How could you use it in this situation? This book will show you.

Hey, Where's Your Projector?

Even if your slides are in order and there are no last-minute changes required, you're not out of the woods yet. Not by a long shot. Did you bring a projector? Many salespeople who routinely use slides often leave their projectors behind because most conference rooms have a projector mounted on the ceiling. This can be a fatal mistake for those with slide dependencies.

I'll never forget a sales call I had where the meeting was originally scheduled in a conference room with a ceiling-mounted projector. But a board meeting ran long, so we were moved to a smaller room without one. Our prospect's admin dug an 800x600 resolution relic out of the A/V closet that cut off the bottom and right side of my slides! I should have avoided the slides altogether.

—Senior Account Exec, HVAC equipment company in Texas

And who hasn't stood on at least two or three conference room tables trying to get a ceiling-mounted projector to work because the remote was either missing, broken, or out of batteries?

I was in [large telecom] presenting to the CIO and the projector mounted on the ceiling just wouldn't work. When you have the CIO in the room, the help desk people show up pretty darn fast. They climbed on the table, pushed through the ceiling tiles, and found that a rat had chewed through the lines!

—Territory Account Manager, Business Service Management Company

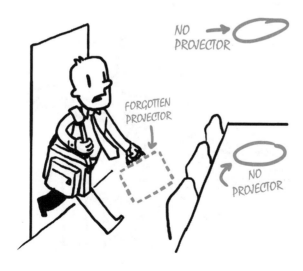

In the Hot Seat

Even the smallest slide projectors have the unfortunate need to cool their projection bulbs. Pity the sad sales soul who has to sit on either side of one.

> *The meeting room was packed and the only seat left was to the side of the projector. I soon realized why. The blast of hot air from the fan quickly soaked through my shirt and I wasn't wearing an undershirt. I joked about not letting anyone see you sweat and got up to move around in front of the screen to try to air myself out. Problem was I had to have one of the attendees advance my slides for me. That day will live in infamy.*
>
> —*Presales Engineer, Medical Equipment and Devices*

You've now got a sense of the history of the slide presentation and its adverse effects for sellers. In the next chapter we'll look at the impact that slide presentations have on sales training.

CHAPTER 2

The Role of Slides in Today's Sales Training

I felt like I was in a war zone. The slides were bombs and the presenters were firing in every direction, but nobody was getting hit. It was just a bunch of loud bangs.

—Business Development Manager, Eastern Region,
large networking firm

The Battle of the Slide Bulge

Have you been to one of these sessions? It's typical product training. All the salespeople are in a room for a full day. Eight hours later they walk out, bleary-eyed and shell-shocked after a long line of presenters has bombarded them with slide presentation after presentation on the latest and greatest products and features. Somewhere in the barrage of slides there should be something that connects those features and functions to value for the customer but, sad to say, this is not the standard.

Slides have negative impacts that reach far beyond the sales meetings with buyers that we described in Chapter 1. Unfortunately, slides are also the cornerstone of how marketing and sales enablement teams equip salespeople with critical knowledge. Salespeople learn the skills they need to do their jobs effectively through slides. And slides are the way the organization communicates to salespeople about the latest and greatest products and solutions. The key phrase here is "communicates *to* them" instead of "communicates *with* them."

Studies show that people retain less than 20 percent of what is presented to them using slides. The "first three slides and last three slides" retention rule—which is scientifically proven—is in full effect. Later in this book you'll learn about the science that shows how passive forms of slide-based selling and slide-based training result in poor retention, poor motivation, and therefore poor results.

Another reason slide presentations are badly suited for sales training, as well as selling, is that they are limitless. By this we mean there are no generally accepted, hard and fast rules on how many slides are consumable by an audience within a specific amount of time, or on how much content is permissible on *each* slide. If there were, whiteboard selling probably wouldn't be such an attractive alternative.

One of the most frustrating things about slide-based training is that the information is transferred to sales reps in such a way that it can't actually be used to facilitate customer conversations. Most of the time, slide-based training becomes a pure transfer of knowledge process rather than equipping sales reps with the critical skills and knowledge they need to hold effective, value-driven conversations with both their company and their customers.

The Slide Agenda from Hell

Does the following sales training agenda look familiar?

	Monday	Tuesday	Wednesday
8:00 AM	**[product name]:** Product overview *Presenter. [name] Sr. Production Marketing Manager*	**[product name]:** Product overview *Presenter. [name] Sr. Production Marketing Manager*	**[product name]:** Product overview *Presenter. [name] Sr. Production Marketing Manager*
9:00 AM	**[product name]:** Product overview *Presenter. [name] Sr. Production Marketing Manager*	**[product name]:** Product overview *Presenter. [name] Sr. Production Marketing Manager*	**[product name]:** Product overview *Presenter. [name] Sr. Production Marketing Manager*
10:00 AM	**[product name]:** Product overview *Presenter. [name] Sr. Production Marketing Manager*	**[product name]:** Product overview *Presenter. [name] Sr. Production Marketing Manager*	**[product name]:** Product overview *Presenter. [name] Sr. Production Marketing Manager*
11:00 AM	**[product name]:** Product overview *Presenter. [name] Sr. Production Marketing Manager*	**[product name]:** Product overview *Presenter. [name] Sr. Production Marketing Manager*	**[product name]:** Product overview *Presenter. [name] Sr. Production Marketing Manager*

It's no wonder salespeople need a stiff drink after a day like this (and this is just the morning agenda!). It's hard enough to retain information from just one of these presentations, let alone five or six or more.

Because these types of training sessions are for the most part noninteractive (with the exception of a five-minute Q&A session at the end), attendees are easily distracted by IMs and e-mails that arrive on their personal devices. If there are no repercussions from management for dozing off or replying to e-mail (after all, it's too dark in the room to see who's not paying attention), it's just too tempting to get distracted.

Not only is this type of training noninteractive, it is nonactionable. What are the expectations? What is a salesperson supposed to do with the information he or she has acquired after training like this?

It's the Norm

Each year, sales organizations large and small congregate at conference centers or headquarters in order to, among other things, get briefed on new products. Slide-based training is the norm for how to do this. For large events, the expense to bring everyone together can be astronomical—in some cases $10,000 or more per attendee (when factoring in travel, accommodation, and other event costs such as conference space, catering, and entertainment). If you accept the premise that only a small fraction of the information contained in a PowerPoint presentation is retained long-term, aside from the benefits of team building and awards dinners, your sales effectiveness dollars are not being put to good use at these meetings.

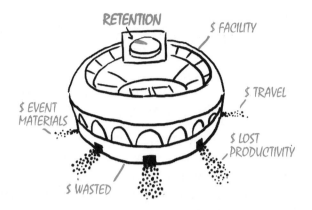

The Typical Annual Kickoff

We recently worked with a large software company that was planning its global annual kickoff, with more than 2,000 sales personnel flying in from more than 20 countries. The cost represented a significant percentage of the annual sales operations budget. Year after year, the agenda of the kickoff didn't change much. It always had the following key elements:

- Opening session
- Product sessions (slide presentations)
- Sales methodology training (some hands-on role playing)
- Awards dinners
- Motivational speaker
- Team building activity (treasure hunt, etc.)
- Closing session

Sales methodology training can be money well spent, assuming it is broadly adoptable, repeatable, and has the right level of accountability and measurement. To their credit, broad-spectrum methodologies that include elements such as organizational mapping, account management best practices, negotiation skills, and so on, usually involve hands-on role plays and scenarios, which help facilitate learning and retention. The weak link in an agenda like the one above, however, is the product presentation component of the sales meeting.

Later we will discuss how we helped this very same organization free itself from slide training jail and move to interactive, memorable, and *effective* sales training and enablement for important sales meetings and kickoffs. We worked closely with the marketing organization to change the way it created and delivered content during the training sessions.

Where Did That Slide Come From?

Even if slide handouts, binders, or laminated sales tools are handed out at the end of day-long presentations, these materials are most likely "round-filed," lost, or put on a shelf to gather dust.

Sometimes presenters will hand out memory sticks at the end of their presentations, or post them to intranets. You may think your sales and marketing messages are locked down when you deliver the slide deck to your sales force and partners. But then the presentation mysteriously morphs and transforms itself as it makes its way around the organization, changed in a way that violates corporate guidelines. Some slides simply disappear, while others, often home grown, are inserted. Before you know it, a completely different message is being communicated to your potential buyers, one that could actually *harm* your brand and identity in the marketplace.

Slide-Fry Your Brain Online

Slides also play heavily in the way online training is conducted for a sales force regardless of size and industry. Internal webinars and other web meetings typically involve a remote version of in-person training—marketing or training personnel presenting slides. There is even more risk of poor retention with these types of training since there is no way to prevent attendees from "alt-tabbing" away from the presentation to do e-mail and other tasks. Online curriculums are also jam-packed with slides stored in learning management systems.

Maintaining online, slide-based learning also becomes a challenge for every training organization. The time and cost required to develop, redevelop, and even just tweak content can very quickly become a drain on resources. Version control can get out of hand, and with the multiple systems, intranets, and individual hard drives where online materials are stored, accessed, and distributed, it can become impossible to ensure that sales reps are using the most up-to-date content.

We hope we've convinced you that slides have the potential to be as damaging to sales training programs as they are to sales calls.

CHAPTER 3

Self-Assessment

Are You Slide-Addicted?

At this point in the book you should be convinced that using slides to communicate internally and with customers and prospects might not be the best approach. And maybe you're even ready to learn a new way. But first, here's a question—how hard will it be to let go of using slides? Are you hopelessly addicted to them?

We've put together a quick assessment to help you find out. Because sales and marketing may have their own special relationship with slides, there's one assessment to use if you're in sales, and another if you're in marketing.

If you're in (or manage) sales:

1. When you see the ad for the thin and light slide projector in *SkyMall* magazine on your flight, you:
   - (a) Turn the page to look at the new food processor being advertised
   - (b) Think it's kind of cool but your sales office already has some older ones
   - (c) Start feeling your palms sweat
   - (d) Purchase in-flight Internet to place the order
2. When building or playing a slide presentation, you:
   - (a) Have trouble figuring out how to get it to play in slide show mode
   - (b) Know where to find the slide animations tab but have never used animations
   - (c) Creatively combine swirl, wipe, and fade bullet builds
   - (d) Actually know how to show slide notes on *your screen* but only *slides* on the projector
3. If the only customer conference room with a projector is unavailable, you:
   - (a) Shrug your shoulders and ask, "Do you have a whiteboard?"
   - (b) Are relieved that you have paper handouts of your presentation
   - (c) Request to reschedule the meeting, giving the first reason you can think of
   - (d) Pull out the thin and light projector you bought on *SkyMall* magazine
4. If your customer starts checking his/her smartphone during your PowerPoint sales presentation, you:
   - (a) Switch off the projector, turn on the lights, and ask, "May I use your whiteboard?"

(b) Lose focus on your presentation and become slightly agitated

(c) Start going faster through your slides to regain attention

(d) Raise your voice to refocus your customer on your presentation

5. If your PC is incompatible or doesn't work correctly with the customer's projector, you:

   (a) Do nothing. You didn't bring a PC, just a set of dry erase markers to present a whiteboard story

   (b) Fiddle with the PC and projector settings to try to fix them

   (c) Ask to use the customer's laptop instead

   (d) Pull out the backup PC you brought just in case (with the presentation preloaded)

If you're in marketing:

1. When putting together product information for sales, you:

   (a) Use PowerPoint sparingly and complement it with podcasts, internal blogs, collaboration tools, and videos of product managers using whiteboards you helped design

   (b) Use a lot of PowerPoint, but use visual images with just a few words

   (c) Use a lot of PowerPoint but have a rule of no more than 20 words per slide, 5 bullets or less, and always using the "build" feature

   (d) Open up a dozen different slide presentations for source content

2. When giving PowerPoint presentations at sales trainings, you:

   (a) Don't use it. Instead, you use an interactive, hands-on activity to teach the content

   (b) Use it only to support a panel-based discussion with sales representatives and product managers

   (c) Prepare printouts with notes pages for the participants that exactly match your presentation delivery

   (d) Provide printouts with note pages plus a thumb drive with the presentation on it

3. When you shop at an electronics store, you:
   (a) Browse a variety of electronic sections including home entertainment
   (b) Look through the business productivity software section
   (c) Purchase some PowerPoint templates
   (d) Clean out the clip art section
4. When a co-worker asks for help sprucing up his or her PowerPoint presentations, you:
   (a) Apologize and say you don't use it much and so probably are not the best person to help
   (b) Suggest eight other people in the department who would be better candidates for helping
   (c) Modestly agree to offer up your PowerPoint skills
   (d) Run-walk rapidly over to their cube and insist on helping right then and there
5. When using a friend's home computer with an older version of PowerPoint, you:
   (a) Can't tell the difference
   (b) Become slightly annoyed that you can't find certain menu items
   (c) Have no problem since you are an expert on all versions
   (d) Insist on downloading a trial copy of the latest version to their machine

Scoring

Whichever test you took (sales or marketing), score yourself:

For each question you answered "a" give yourself one point.
For each question you answered "b" give yourself two points.
For each question you answered "c" give yourself three points.
For each question you answered "d" give yourself four points.

If you scored 5–8:

You belong in the Whiteboarding Hall of Fame.

If you scored 9–12:

You're well on the road to recovery.

If you scored 13–16:

Have a co-worker hide your projector where you'll never find it.

If you scored 17–20:

Do not pass Go. Do not collect $200. Go directly to PowerPoint Jail.

PART 2

The Visual Selling Opportunity

CHAPTER 4

The Power of the Pen

Let me assure you here and now, that I have been using this new approach to whiteboarding since returning from New Hire Training in the past two weeks—with a 100 percent success rate. As you can imagine, walking into strong competitor incumbent accounts, the clients are very hostile and apprehensive, but every time I have run through the whiteboard, the walls start to crumble and break down, and our organization is seen in a very different light.

—Major Accounts Rep, Asia Pacific Region,
large data management firm

Since you've made it to Part 2, there's a good chance you agree there's no better way to torpedo a sales call than to plug in a projector and start presenting a bunch of slides—the proverbial "show up and throw up." There's no second chance to create a first impression. You only have one opportunity to differentiate yourself, to stand out from the crowd, and be someone who can add value and solve problems. So how can you become a partner *with* your customers rather than a salesperson *to* them?

The answer is the *power of the pen*—the power of a salesperson of any tenure or experience to get up in front of a C-level buyer and deliver a visually rich and interactive presentation with complete confidence and command of the material.

"Power of the pen" isn't a term we created; in fact, it's been around for centuries. It comes from the age-old adage, "The pen is mightier than the sword." According to Wikipedia, the saying was coined by English author Edward Bulwer-Lytton in 1839 for his play *Richelieu; Or the Conspiracy*. The subject of the play was Cardinal Richelieu, whose famous line in Act II, scene II, cemented the term in popular culture:

> True, This! —Beneath the rule of men entirely great,
> The pen is mightier than the sword. Behold
> The arch-enchanters wand!—itself a nothing!—
> But taking sorcery from the master-hand
> To paralyse the Caesars, and to strike
> The loud earth breathless!—Take away the sword
> States can be saved without it!

Let's try a modern-day revision in the context of selling:

> If sales management is getting on your case,
> The dry erase marker is always better than slides.
> Let's face it—
> A good whiteboarder's marker by itself is nothing
> But if you're a powerful visual storyteller
> You'll really connect with your buyer, and win the deal
> And you'll tee up huge enterprise deals!—Get rid of your slide projector
> You'll win plenty of sales without it!

Note: An illustration of Cardinal Richelieu trying in vain to lift a sword, by H. A. Ogden, 1892, from *The Works of Edward Bulwer-Lytton*.

"I Don't Need a Sword—I Already Whiteboard"

High-dollar salespeople and sales engineers have been whiteboarding for decades. What we advocate is structure, process, and whiteboarding ingredients to turn the pen from a shotgun into a devastating, laser-guided competitive weapon that will leave your slide-addicted competition in the dust.

A couple of years into our business, we worked with a company that had a very heavy whiteboarding culture. Everyone was whiteboarding, and slides were frowned upon. A few weeks after going through our whiteboard training, a sales engineering VP from our customer e-mailed us:

> [NAME] was the model for whiteboarding before we discovered your company. I took a couple of photos of some whiteboards he did; something told me they would be useful one day. When he was done with this particular whiteboard attempt it looked like an abstract expressionist painting. I followed him while he was doing it but had no idea what any of it meant when he was done. Fortunately, he has huge shoulders and can take being the anti-role model. Now he and his team are training our Channel Partner SEs on the whiteboards done right and they're furiously eating them up as fast as we can deliver them.

It's not enough to take a marker to a whiteboard. Even if salespeople and other field personnel are big whiteboarders, they probably lack critical whiteboard story design and delivery best practices.

"I Don't Need Slides *or* a Whiteboard"

Some of the most successful and seasoned sales professionals tend not to be big fans of slides, but they have no inclination to use a whiteboard either. These sellers will sit down in an executive's office and start talking about kids, family, and common interests, then subtly ease into a dialogue around business challenges, opportunities, and consensus on next steps.

Eventually, however, even senior-level buyers will want to know "where's the beef"—they still need to get some sense of what your solution actually looks like in their own environment and how it pertains to their unique business needs and current challenges. This is when selling value with nothing more than a pen and a drawing surface proves so effective.

Following whiteboard training, these strategic salespeople consistently report, "I never thought I would want to do that, let alone be *able* to do it."

Be Different!—And Lighten Your Load at the Same Time

The power of the pen can have an impact even before the caps come off and the smell of dry erase ink hits the nose. Think about this scenario: You leave for your sales calls with two things and two things only—a set of brand-new dry erase markers (red, green, black, blue) with a rubber band around them, and your camera phone. That's it. No briefcase, no computer bag, no day planner, no notepad, no nothing. Why? Because with the markers and your camera phone, you have everything you need. Today you'll find a whiteboard in almost every meeting room and office you'll encounter. The whiteboard and your markers enable you to conduct the interactive discussion and to note your customer's current situation, challenges, questions, and next steps. The camera phone allows you to capture the entire discussion for a variety of uses after the sales call (we'll discuss this more in Chapter 27). You don't need to have anything else.

Let's continue the scenario. The first thing you do when you sit down for the meeting is to conspicuously place your pens and your phone on the table. You do this to make a point. Chances are your customers will immediately notice that something is different.

When we go to meetings to talk about our whiteboard selling techniques, our customers chuckle and say, "I get it—just the pens." And we reply, "That's right. The reason we are here today is to show you how we will enable every single member of your entire sales channel to do what we are about to do—but with your own story." And they nod. They get it.

By whiteboarding, whether you are the first or last vendor to meet with your prospect, you can smile at the thought of those "slide jockeys" at your competition struggling with laptops, projectors, remotes, and projection screens that won't come down.

When you walk in with just your pens and your smartphone, you are communicating to your customer that you are going to really talk to them and engage in an interactive conversation. They know you are confident in your skills.

CHAPTER 5

The Science Behind Whiteboard Selling

Grabbing the Pen, Not the Computer

You want your customer to engage with you. Have you ever been in a meeting with a customer who grabs a marker and starts writing on the board? You probably have. How many times have you been in a meeting where the customer grabs your laptop and creates or shows slides? Not very often!

V. S. Ramachandran gave a TED talk on mirror neurons.[1] Mirror neurons are special neurons in the brain that cause us to imitate what we see. If you are writing on a whiteboard, it will be more likely for your customer to grab a pen and start writing, too. And if they do, then you are having much more interaction than if you are presenting a slide deck and your customer is just listening.

Markers are interactive; slides are not. You want to engage your customer in the dialogue. There's something very powerful about graphically depicting solution knowledge without slides to prop you up. When your prospect grabs the pen and says, "We do it this way today," you and your customer are on the way to creating a shared vision around how your products and solutions can address their specific business requirements in a way your competition can't.

Keeping Attention

Research by Kalina Christoff, Associate Professor at the Brain Research Center, University of British Columbia, shows that everyone's mind wanders more than one-third of the time.[2] With whiteboarding, your customer will be less likely to have a wandering mind. As Christoff puts it, they become "on task."

When you are drawing on a whiteboard, you are physically moving. The human brain is programmed to pay attention to movement.[3] Every time you draw something on the whiteboard you bring your customer's attention back to the whiteboard, even if the mind has started to

---

[1]V. S. Ramachandran, "The Neurons That Shaped Civilization," TED Talk, 2010, http://bit.ly/aaiXba.

[2]Kalina Christoff, "Experience Sampling during fMRI Reveals Default Network and Executive System Contributions to Mind Wandering." Proceedings of the National Academy of Sciences (2009).

[3]Susan Weinschenk, *100 Things Every Presenter Needs to Know About People* (San Francisco: Peachpit, 2012).

wander. PowerPoint is more static—not much is moving. It's easier for your prospects' minds to wander when they are watching a PowerPoint presentation.

In addition to mind wandering, people can have a hard time listening and reading at the same time. According to presentation expert Susan Weinschenk, when people are trying to listen to you present but are also looking at a slide with lots of text or a complicated graphic, they have multiple sensory channels competing.[4]

When you draw on a whiteboard, the drawing enhances what is being said, so the two channels work together. Also, because you can stop drawing, you can control when people are looking (visual channel) and when they are listening (auditory channel).

Bite-Size Chunks

People process information better when it is in bite-sized chunks. The term that psychologists use for this is Progressive Disclosure.[5]

---

[4]Ibid.

[5]Ibid.

Because you are drawing, you are automatically creating small chunks, as opposed to a PowerPoint where you push one button and an entire confusing slide with lots of text or a complicated graphic can appear all at once.

The Power of Stories

People process information best in story format. Research by Singer, et al.[6] and in a report in the *New York Times*[7] now shows that when people listen to or read stories, their brains are active as though they are acting out the story. For example, if you read a story and someone in the story is running, you will show activity in your motor cortex. It's as though you are running, too.

When you use a whiteboard you will have a tendency to talk in terms of stories, instead of just data. You can't just read the slides. You have to put the information in your own terms. This will make the material more interesting, more story-like, and, in turn, will help your listener process the information more deeply.

---

[6]T. Singer, B. Seymour, J. O'Doherty, H. Kaube, J. D. Dolan, and C. Frith, "Empathy for Pain Involves the Affective but Not Sensory Component of Pain," *Science* 303 (2004):1157–1162.

[7]"Your Brain on Fiction," *New York Times*, March 17, 2012, nyti.ms/J9xjcg.

CHAPTER 6

Old Disciplines, New Behaviors

By changing the approach from slides to whiteboarding, my customers get the vision. The reaction is typically, "I get what you are trying to do." The content used to be in a bunch of slides. The whiteboard just lets me frame it in a different way, as a cohesive story. The customer is engaged, they aren't messing around with their devices. And they always say, "Let me take a picture of the whiteboard." I've never had a customer say, "I want to take a picture of that slide."

—Technology Specialist, large software company

With "power of the pen" as a rallying cry, let's look at a new way of selling, using visuals to do five things.

1. **Earn the right** to be in front of your customers by confirming their existing situation.
2. **Show your customers you know how to listen** to them before talking about what you can offer, by using the whiteboard to diagnose and spur interactivity.

3. **Demonstrate knowledge ownership** and position yourself as a trusted advisor by conveying your products' and solutions' *unique and differentiated* value proposition on a whiteboard (or any other writing surface) in a confident, compelling, and consistent fashion.
4. **Be situationally fluent** and take the conversation wherever it needs to go at the moment.
5. **Close for next steps** to drive the opportunity forward.

Perhaps you're thinking, "This is nothing new—I've been through this a dozen times in various sales trainings and methodologies; listen, diagnose, ask questions, consult, adapt—I've heard it all before."

And you'd be right—to a degree. These five sales disciplines—*on their own*—are in no way groundbreaking. But throw in some pens and a drawing surface and they take on new meaning and provide new opportunities. In other words, the whiteboarding discipline doesn't replace or conflict with a given sales methodology—it puts it on steroids.

Let's take a closer look at how these five disciplines play out in the world of selling with visuals.

Earn the Right and You'll Earn the Business

When we start out working with our customers, one of the first things we ask to see are their existing PowerPoint sales presentations. Next, we interview some of their salespeople to understand how they use them. Typically, salespeople aren't doing extensive customizations from presentation to presentation. They change the date on the opening slide, change names, and sometimes they insert, remove, or reposition slides, depending on the specific product interests of the customer. Why aren't they making more customizations? Are these salespeople inherently lazy? Some might be, but it's not just inherent laziness that prevents more customization.

Know Your Ingredients Before You Cook

PowerPoint is so good at making us much lazier than we already are. PowerPoint is to presenting what microwave ovens are to cooking. Why bother messing up your kitchen or learning to cook when you can just press "Start"? Do I have what it takes to be a good cook? Yes, probably. But why should I bother? If I'm a salesperson, I have a million other things on my plate—forecast calls, sales force tools to update, existing customer issues, and on and on. It's just too easy to pull out the microwaveable meal.

Salespeople who whiteboard or otherwise draw with visuals don't have this luxury. They need to know the ingredients—their prospect's business and major industry trends—before they start cooking. This requires doing some extra homework, but the benefits far outweigh the extra effort. If you begin a whiteboard discussion by establishing and writing up on the board what you already know (or think you know) about your prospect's current situation, business objectives, initiatives, and relevant market trends, the credibility boost will be enormous. You'll immediately earn the right to continue the dialogue to create a shared vision.

In later chapters, you'll learn possible whiteboard discussion structures and story flows, and how they should be developed. But the best whiteboarders take their company's standard whiteboard storyboards and create customer-specific templates before each and every sales call. They prep the opening steps of the whiteboard with their prospect's current situation by sketching it out on a piece of paper or on an erasable laminate. Then they practice this opening three or four times before they leave for the meeting. It's one thing to show your customers you know the most important elements of their business and existing situation. It's another thing entirely if you can write all of this up on the whiteboard from memory.

Bringing it home:

- Use the whiteboard to confirm what you know about the prospect's current situation and business objectives
- Visually demonstrate your knowledge of industry trends to enhance credibility
- Build a practice sheet with customized opening steps of each whiteboard

Prove You're Listening. "Shhhhh—These Whiteboards Have Ears!"

There's not a sales methodology ever invented that doesn't scream from the mountain tops, "Show your customers you know how to listen to them so you can understand what keeps them up at night, diagnose pain, and further qualify the opportunity." Or something like that.

Because you've used the whiteboard to share what you already know and confirm whether you're right, you are in a great position to ask more questions, do the listening and qualification, and capture your discovery as the discussion progresses.

Using a whiteboard to drive interactivity is exponentially more effective than sitting across from your customer and taking page after page of notes as you ask questions. How does the customer know exactly what you are writing down? This disconnects you from your customer. The whiteboard as a listening tool requires you to be selective in what you capture, focusing on the most salient points. You no longer need to stress about having to write down every single word your customer says.

You'll also demonstrate a new physical dimension of customer intimacy by standing up at the whiteboard and capturing input for everyone in a well-lit room to see. The act of standing and drawing has a subtle yet powerful psychological impact. If the customer sees you writing what you are hearing, it signals that you are acknowledging their input and concerns. Not to mention that your entire body is in motion. Your arm is moving. The prospect can't really "check out" the same way they can if you are sitting across a conference table taking copious notes, or worse, presenting slides.

Bringing it home:

- Use the whiteboard to diagnose and drive interactivity
- Be selective when capturing customer input on the whiteboard
- Use physicality and gesturing to show you're listening

Be the Subject Matter Expert! You'll Never Write Something on the Whiteboard That's Not in Your Head

> *His knowledge on that topic is only PowerPoint deep.*
>
> —Anonymous US Army Major

Before you even think about getting in front of a customer or prospect to begin whiteboarding, you have to be comfortable with the skill of confirming and diagnosing with a pen, and you also must have complete "knowledge ownership" of the solution or service you are positioning. Without slides behind you as a crutch, you now have no excuse for *not* knowing your products and solutions inside and out. There will never be a case where some magical force takes control of your pen and you draw something on the whiteboard that's not in your head.

Better knowledge ownership shows the customer you are not only an expert in the field, but more of a trusted partner than just someone trying to hawk wares. When you become a trusted partner, you shorten the sales cycle and prevent lengthy product comparisons and "bake-offs."

Yesterday [name] closed a deal at a new logo at [an international tire company]. The sales cycle started in early December with a Request for Proposal and subsequent shortlist. We then had one main presentation where [name] used a whiteboard based on the sales kick-off enablement, and using their annual report as initiatives and local customer stories. At the end the CIO took a picture of the diagram and from that checked out a reference—they had originally planned a proof of concept which was avoided and the deal closed against [competitor] within two weeks. Not saying all will be as easy but it's a nice story. Well done!!

—[name] Area VP

Knowledge ownership shortens the sales cycle and acts as a deadly differentiator against the competition. It also helps you rely less on technical or presales resources during the early stages of the sales process. Presales teams want to be leveraged in the right way and participate in qualified sales opportunities. If you can conduct initial sales calls without slides—using whiteboarding instead—then you can be more flexible when it comes to scheduling meetings. And that can compress sales cycles.

In the earlier story from the field, here's what happened after using the whiteboard in a structured fashion:

- The salesperson heavily researched the prospect's business using publicly available information
- Local case studies and references were integrated into the story
- The whiteboard lived on because the CIO took a picture of it
- The salesperson successfully differentiated himself from the competition
- The sales cycle was shortened considerably

Later in the book we will detail exactly how this salesperson was able to have such a dramatic impact on sales results using the whiteboarding best practices and approaches we advocate.

Bringing it home:

- Build trust with whiteboarding and you'll avoid bake-offs and proofs of concepts
- Reduce dependency on precious presales and SME resources through self-sufficiency in initial sales calls
- Shorten the sales cycle

Be Flexible—Go with the Flow

I'm terrible at story and structure, but I'm not so bad at writing dialogue.

—Steve Buscemi

The term "situational fluency" in the context of sales means a lot of things to a lot of people. From a strategic, solution-selling level, it could mean that salespeople should know what makes their customers tick and exactly why they need the salesperson's solutions. What exactly is it about the customer's current situation that makes the solution a perfect fit now, instead of in six months or a year? In this context, situational fluency also means being able to set the agenda for the next steps in the sales process.

Situational fluency means something different when you are making a presentation to your customer at a specific time and place—in the moment. You need to think on your feet and take the temperature of your prospect, changing direction based on what you are hearing and who you are hearing it from, and do so *instantly*. It means going a level up, down, across, or knowing when to stop the conversation altogether by setting up next steps.

If we define situational fluency as the ability to make in the moment adaptations depending on where your customer takes the discussion, then slides will fail. You *cannot* accomplish situational fluency with slides, even if you have an hour's worth of advance notice. This is where the "I'll get to that in five slides" syndrome kicks in. The whiteboard, on the other hand, is a match made in heaven when it comes to situational fluency because you can jump to the right part of the story, omitting elements that do not apply, or adding ones that do. When you are using "in the moment" situational fluency, you can bring in relevant customer stories, proof points, and references depending on the trajectory of the conversation.

The physical nature of the whiteboard also comes into play here and increases situational fluency. Not only can your prospects pick up on your body language, but you can also pick up on theirs. With the lights turned up instead of dimmed for slides, you can get good eye contact with them and gauge body language and level of engagement as you progress through the story. You can then pivot and navigate to a different topic based on your prospect's reactions.

Bringing it home:

- Be situationally fluent at both a strategic and in-the-moment level
- Get an instant read on your prospect's body language as you write on the whiteboard
- Be prepared to pivot and maneuver within the whiteboard structure and flow

Close for Next Steps. Only Then Put the Cap on the Pen

Successful salespeople don't leave a meeting until they have secured next steps. These can include additional meetings with other stakeholders, in-depth product evaluations, assessments, and demonstrations. Because whiteboarding helps you gain trusted advisor status, you might be able to avoid some of these steps altogether. Depending on the specific sales situation, though, you may have next steps, and the whiteboard is a particularly effective way to establish and agree on what those next steps are.

Instead of just writing down the next steps on a notepad or organizer, you can capture them on the whiteboard for everyone to see. By "memorializing" these next steps on the whiteboard and getting physical acknowledgment from your prospect through a head nod as you write, you have essentially made a pact with them that they will feel obligated to make good on.

Every sales methodology has its own style or prescription of how to ask for next steps. One that we have observed to be effective is:

"If what you see on the whiteboard resonates, I'd like to propose some next steps and capture them on the whiteboard. Would that be okay?"

In the following chapters we'll demonstrate how multiple whiteboard discussion frameworks and stories can support situational fluency, establish trusted advisor status, and shorten the sales cycle.

PART 3

What Exactly Is a Whiteboard for Sales?

CHAPTER 7

When to Use Whiteboards in the Sales Process

You may not need all of the whiteboard types we discuss in this book. How many and which ones you need depends on the unique sales situation or sales process you use. While we are clearly strong advocates of using whiteboarding instead of PowerPoint, in some cases slides—and *not* whiteboards—may play a useful role at various points in the sales process.

We will review each whiteboard type in detail in Chapter 8, but generally speaking you use Qualification and Discovery Whiteboards early in the sales process, and Closing Whiteboards later. But you can use Why Change, Solution, Competitive, and Business Case Whiteboards situationally.

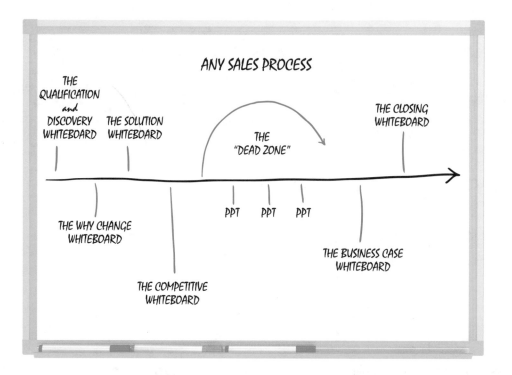

The figure above identifies where in the general flow of the sales process you would typically use each type of whiteboard. The "Dead Zone" is the part of the sales process that, we hope, can be removed altogether. It involves in-depth product evaluations, proofs of concepts, and "bake-offs." This is a place where PowerPoint can be effective in demonstrating product features and functions, and complex schematics, architectures, or workflows that whiteboards are simply not well tailored to.

Your goal should always be to use whiteboarding as early in the sales process as possible. This positions you as a thought leader and trusted advisor. That, in turn, compresses the sales cycle, removes the extra steps, and keeps the projectors back at the office.

Sales Process Agnostic

Most organizations have a particular sales process. How does the use of these various whiteboards fit into whatever sales process your organization has? We've mentioned before that whiteboarding is agnostic to, and integrates with, any sales process. Here's an example:

According to Wikipedia, there are a couple of generic sales processes that are representative of many packaged methodologies, and that vary from company to company. Below we've indicated where you could use different whiteboard types within a typical sales process. Notice that the mapping is approximate and offers a lot of flexibility in how and when you can leverage the various whiteboard types.

Sales Process Example #1
1. Initial contact
2. Application of initial fit criteria
3. Sales lead
4. Need identification (Qualification and Discovery Whiteboard, and Why Change Whiteboard)
5. Qualified prospect
6. Proposal (Solution Whiteboard and Business Case Whiteboard)
7. Negotiation (Business Case Whiteboard)
8. Closing (Business Case Whiteboard and/or Closing Whiteboard)
9. Deal transaction

Sales Process Example #2
1. Prospecting/initial contact (Qualification and Discovery Whiteboard)
2. Preapproach; planning the sale
3. Approach
4. Need assessment (Qualification and Discovery Whiteboard, and Why Change Whiteboard)
5. Presentation (Solution Whiteboard and Business Case Whiteboard)

6. Meeting objections (Competitive Whiteboard)
7. Gaining commitment (Business Case Whiteboard and Closing Whiteboard)
8. Follow-up

You can see that various whiteboard types can be used regardless of sales process, and even in multiple stages. Another example of situational fluency is to determine which whiteboards are effective at different parts of the sales process, depending on the unique sales situation and customer buying cycle.

The Whiteboard Lunch-and-Learn

For those old-school sales professionals, lunch-and-learns are a tried-and-true mechanism to gain exposure to a broad and diverse audience within your target account. You can replace PowerPoint with white-boarding, and achieve all the benefits we've already discussed, but in front of a larger audience.

We recently worked with a customer that sells, among other things, telepresence and video conferencing solutions. This technology allows people in geographically dispersed locations to interact as if they were in the same conference room. We heard about one case where a salesperson located in San Francisco invited 10 or 12 people from a prospect account based in New York to a virtual lunch-and-learn. The salesperson ordered pizza to show up at the precise time when the attendees in New York were seated around the conference room. Using the telepresence technology, the salesperson stood at the whiteboard in San Francisco and presented the story, which was broadcast in high definition to his customers in New York.

In the following chapters we'll look at each type of whiteboard in depth, providing real-world examples and giving you the chance to create your own versions through guided activities.

CHAPTER 8

The Major Whiteboard Types

If you're sitting in your minivan, playing your computer-animated films for your children in the backseat, is it the animation that's entertaining you as you drive and listen? No, it's the storytelling. That's why we put so much importance on story. No amount of great animation will save a bad story.

—John Lasseter

So far in this book we have showcased the stories of real salespeople and their experiences with PowerPoint and whiteboarding. Part of the power of whiteboarding is the power of stories. There are plenty of other books that sing the praises of storytelling. Using stories, especially visual stories, creates a shared vision and helps to sell more and bigger deals, faster. But using whiteboards to tell stories is just part of the picture. An effective sales whiteboard needs to be more than a narrative—it should also be a discussion framework that supports a two-way knowledge transfer. This discussion framework builds out step-by-step, while still allowing for situational fluency if the discussion changes course. It has predesignated areas to capture customer meeting objectives, feedback, and next steps. This "discussion map" is critical to keeping the dialogue moving to create a shared vision and progress the sales cycle.

In this section, we will describe at a high level the key whiteboard types. In later sections we'll describe the basic design points of a whiteboard and the associated content.

The Whiteboard Army Knife

We identify a total of six different types of whiteboards that can be used in different situations and at different stages that work with whatever sales process you adhere to. These are:

1. Qualification and Discovery Whiteboards
2. Why Change Whiteboards
3. Solution Whiteboards
4. Competitive Whiteboards
5. Business Case Whiteboards
6. Closing Whiteboards

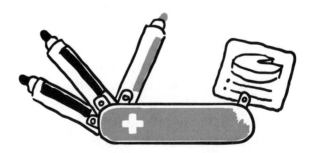

You may be thinking, "Wow, that's a lot of whiteboards I need to learn to be effective without using PowerPoint!" The reality is that you will rarely ever need to deliver all or even more than one of these whiteboards, depending on the unique sales situation. Keep in mind, they come in many different forms and flavors, and that regardless of which type of whiteboard you are using, *they must all drive to specific next steps and actions* that move the sales process forward.

Qualification and Discovery Whiteboards

These whiteboards are used to assess the value of a lead to see if it has merit to become a qualified opportunity. Qualification and Discovery Whiteboards are also effective in providing a chance to identify the prospect's existing challenges and business objectives, and to ensure there is a sufficient amount of alignment with your offerings.

Next Step/Action

By gathering important information about a prospect's current situation, Qualification and Discovery Whiteboards lay the groundwork for a Why Change Whiteboard or a Solution Whiteboard, or at the very least, the need for more discovery with other stakeholders via a phone conference or web meeting.

Why Change Whiteboards

Many buyers know they need to evolve how they operate their businesses and are therefore actively in pursuit of solutions or products to address new objectives, initiatives, and projects to help them become more competitive and grow. These buyers are "in the market," so to speak, yet unfortunately they are in the minority. The most successful salespeople earn the kind of money they do because they are hunters and not farmers. Farmers take orders from in-the-market buyers. Hunters generate new demand for their offerings among prospects who are not convinced they need to change the status quo. Even if a Qualification and Discovery Whiteboard does not signal a sales opportunity that is ripe for the picking, hunters will not be dissuaded from pursuit.

Why Change Whiteboards help farmers become hunters by providing a structured discussion framework to help these status quo buyers understand the risk of inaction.

Next Step/Action

Once a prospect has seen the light and that change is needed, a Solution Whiteboard provides the required detail about your offerings to move the sales process to the next stage.

Solution Whiteboards

Solution Whiteboards are often the most frequently used whiteboard type in the sales process. You've identified a qualified opportunity based on a preliminary alignment of your prospect's business challenges and objectives with your solutions. Or, you've used a Why Change Whiteboard to create the demand for your offering in the mind of your buyer. Now it's time for a more in-depth dialogue and knowledge transfer around how your solutions and services uniquely address your prospect's needs, and where you've had proven success helping other customers.

Solution Whiteboards usually start by confirming what has been learned so far from a Qualification and Discovery Whiteboard, a Why Change Whiteboard, or from other initial discussions you've had with the customer. Solution Whiteboards are designed to answer the question, "So where's the beef?" Now it's time to communicate, "Here's what we do, how we do it, and why we're unique."

In some cases, you can use parts of a Solution Whiteboard in the very same meeting after you have used a Qualification and Discovery or a Why Change Whiteboard. As there is no requirement to present all whiteboard types in any given sales engagement, a Solution Whiteboard may be the first whiteboard you deliver to the customer.

One of the participants from our whiteboard enablement program sent us an e-mail about how she had struck up a conversation with a potential buyer on an airplane. Her seatmate asked her what her company could offer, and she pulled out the air sickness bag from the seat pocket and proceeded to do a rough version of one of her company's Solution Whiteboards. She even captured some of her buyer's unique challenges before handing him the bag to take with him.

Next Step/Action

The next step after a Solution Whiteboard will vary significantly based on the sales situation and type of sales process. The outcome should be to lay the groundwork for a shared vision on how your solutions can uniquely address your prospect's goals and objectives. Ideally, the possible next steps are a proposal and a request to open a purchase order! Next steps might also include presenting a Competitive Whiteboard, in-depth assessments, and a meeting with key stakeholders responsible for further evaluation. In many cases an effectively delivered Solution Whiteboard will lead directly to vendor selection and a closed deal.

Competitive Whiteboards

A Solution Whiteboard isn't always enough to seal the deal, and the prospect may want a head-to-head comparison of how you stack up against a competing vendor or group of vendors. The objective of a Competitive Whiteboard is to clearly and authoritatively demonstrate how your solution is superior across a specific set of criteria that are most important to your prospect. Technical and other presales resources are often involved in the presentation of Competitive Whiteboards.

Next Step/Action

The ideal outcome of presenting this whiteboard is final vendor selection in your favor, avoiding any type of proof of concept or in-depth evaluation.

Business Case Whiteboards

Have you ever had a customer say, "Yes, we believe you have the right solution and we want to look at how we can implement it," but the next thing out of their mouth is, "How am I going to pay for it and how long will it take for me to see ROI (Return on Investment)?" A Business Case Whiteboard provides a clear answer to these types of questions, usually in a quantitative fashion. Business Case Whiteboards are valuable, but they are not always required and they may even slow down the sales process if used at the wrong time and place.

Next Step/Action

Final vendor selection in your favor.

Closing Whiteboards

You've gotten to a point in the sales process where the need is established for your solution, you are the acknowledged first choice, and you've proven how your offerings will pay for themselves. But in many cases, your "champion" or sponsor isn't at the right level to have final budget and signing approval, or someone at a higher level within the organization needs convincing.

Closing Whiteboards are simple whiteboards—sometimes a condensed version of both a Solution Whiteboard and a Business Case Whiteboard—designed to seal the deal. As one of our trainees reported several weeks after training, "My customer loved the whiteboard and plans to use it as the basis for telling the story to the committee that approves their funding."

In some cases, the presentation of a Closing Whiteboard may require the presence and participation of higher-level executives from your sales organization.

Next Step/Action

You should be exhausted by now! The desired outcome is final vendor selection and a Statement of Work or Purchase Order for signature.

In the following chapters we'll provide in-depth explanations and examples of each type of whiteboard.

CHAPTER 9

Whiteboard Case Study

Organizations we work with view their whiteboards as competitive assets and consider them to be highly confidential, so it was difficult to get permission to share them in this book. Therefore, we've created a case study of an imaginary company so we can demonstrate the various whiteboard types in a real-world scenario. The case study business is a refrigerated truck company named Cool Road Trucking. Why have we selected such a seemingly obscure example? Whiteboarding can apply to *any* organization in *any* industry selling *any* products, solutions, and services that have complexity, expense, and deliver significant business value. With the Cool Road case study, we can show the important whiteboard ingredients that are core to the whiteboard selling methodology. The case study is as realistic as possible, but we admit we are no refrigerated trucking experts!

Let's look at some of the key facts about Cool Road and their capabilities. We will use these as examples in the whiteboard templates that we cover in this section.

Company Name: Cool Road Trucking

Cool Road Trucking is the number-three US provider of temperature-controlled trucking capacity. They offer the most technologically advanced fleet of refrigerated equipment, plus a broad network of product handling hubs and consolidation points to ensure the highest levels of on-time delivery and customer satisfaction. Cool Road even offers product sourcing to ensure economies of scale and smooth transition from supplier to end customer.

Cool Road offers refrigerated capacity for pharmaceuticals, confectionary products, dietary products, beverages, healthcare bio-products, and of course, food products. For the purposes of the case study, Cool Road's customer will be a chain of food stores called Foody's Fresh Foods that receives supplies of produce.

Cool Road's Unique Capabilities

Cool Road is differentiated from the competition in a number of ways, and the company trains its sales force to clearly demonstrate how its broad solution is unique in the market.

Full Life Cycle Services

Cool Road doesn't only offer access to a huge fleet of refrigerated trucks; it also provides one of the largest networks of shipment collection points and hubs designed specifically for refrigerated payloads. To ensure rapid resolution of equipment problems and road incidents, the company chooses not to outsource customer service, tracking and monitoring, equipment maintenance, or emergency services. Cool Road also provides end-product sourcing services to cut out the middlemen and ensure consistency of product handling and speed of delivery. This approach provides lower cost "from field to store." Cool Road is differentiated from trucking companies and suppliers that also provide nonrefrigerated cargo, rail capacity, and even shipping containers. A laser focus on refrigerated payloads and surrounding services is what makes Cool Road unique.

One Point of Contact

To support this full life cycle approach, Cool Road provides a single point of contact for all issues related to sourcing, delivery, and monitoring. When any questions arise related to delivery status, product quality, or sourcing terms, customers can contact a dedicated account manager assigned to each customer. The benefit is faster problem resolution and customer satisfaction.

Nationwide Network

Cool Road offers one of the largest networks of temperature-controlled hubs and collection points, with 118 hubs in 36 states. This provides LTL (Less Than Truckload) capability, which enables the collection of smaller refrigerated freight shipments from more suppliers using smaller trucks, and then consolidating those shipments at hubs for transfer to fully loaded semis. Competing carriers offer FTL (Full Truck Load) only, which limits flexibility and leads to delays and increased spoilage, not to mention higher fuel costs.

TempTrust

Most refrigeration control systems are bolted onto existing semis, but Cool Road's temperature control units are built into their equipment to ensure superior temperature control from supplier to destination. These systems are powered by TempTrust technology, which immediately adjusts temperature based on climate changes without driver intervention. Competing solutions simply provide alarm systems that require drivers to manually raise or lower temperature, which leads to delayed and incorrect adjustments.

CleanCool

For customers looking to be "greener," Cool Road offers CleanCool technology, which not only increases efficiency by reducing the energy needs of the cooling systems (leading to cost savings), it also limits emissions of dangerous chemicals and other toxic compounds typical of competing cooling units. Emission reduction levels are measured and tracked for the purpose of benchmarking against industry averages and to comply with regulations.

The Cool Road Advantage

In summary, Cool Road is a lower risk, proven, and more innovative refrigerated trucking solution than any other on the market. Analysts and press agree, as Cool Road was recently awarded *FridgeRoad Magazine's* number-one rating, and a *RideCold Rating* Top Pick.

The majority of the whiteboard templates and examples we share in the following sections are modeled on the Cool Road case study.

Foody's Fresh Food's Current Situation and Challenges

Foody's Fresh Food is Cool Road's prospect in the imaginary sales scenario. A national food store chain undergoing significant growth, Foody's is opening a new store each month across the United States. The chain is seeking to compete with, and steal market share from, premium brands that offer a broader mix and higher quality selection of fresh produce, meat, and seafood. Meanwhile, cost cutting measures are under way to increase profit and shareholder value, requiring competitive pricing and special terms from all suppliers and vendors. To compete, Foody's needs to reduce produce spoilage rates and decrease field-to-store times.

Now let's take a look at the different whiteboard types using the Cool Road case study as an example.

CHAPTER 10

Whiteboard Structure, Flow, Content, and Interaction Points

The fact that the message was built and flowed throughout, and built in a relevant way, made the content easier to internalize, easier to get a grasp on, and then easier for me to personalize going forward.

—Executive Strategist, systems management software company

When you read a book there are certain elements you rely on. There is the content of the book, the words, and the pictures. There is a table of contents that shows you the outline. The author has ordered the ideas, or the narrative, of the story so it makes sense. There is a visual design and layout that help you better understand the content.

A whiteboard for sales has similar elements. Each whiteboard you use during the sales process needs a predetermined structure you can use and then improvise on as needed, depending on how the sales meeting progresses. Each whiteboard dialogue has elements you can count on to help you communicate.

What are the elements of a whiteboard dialogue? One element is *content*—the words and visuals that communicate the unique value of whatever is being sold. Another element of the content is a script associated with each step of the whiteboard, which supports the visuals by providing a talk track. The script is designed to be an example of talking points only, not to be used verbatim by the presenter. The best practice is for the seller to customize the script according to the needs of each customer or prospect, leveraging the concept of situational fluency.

As with any story or narrative, a whiteboard for sales has a number of logical steps or break points in the content that act like sections and chapters in a book. These steps and break points make up the *flow* of the visual story.

Finally, every whiteboard designed for selling must include a number of key *interaction points* when, in addition to drawing and talking, the presenter pauses to engage with the customer or prospect.

Types of Interaction Points

There are three key types of interaction points:

1. *Confirmations*—Confirmation interaction points demonstrate your knowledge of your prospect's unique business situation. A confirmation allows you to recap what you already know (or think you know!) about their existing needs, challenges, and near-term initiatives.
2. *Open-Ended Questions*—Open-ended questions engage the customer. You use questions to get feedback on what is being discussed, to learn more, and to keep the discussion interactive. Remember, a whiteboard for sales is designed to encourage a two-way information exchange. Depending on which sales methodology or process you are using, you can leverage different questioning models. Questions should be open-ended to keep the dialogue

moving. Yes/no questions can result in awkward pauses following a "no" answer from a prospect. You will want to align the questions with the topics being discussed at each whiteboard step.

3. *Objection Reframes*—As with any sales presentation, customers will challenge the whiteboard presenter with objections and questions, either to dig deeper into certain topics, to test the presenter, or to regurgitate competitive landmines planted by other vendors. When you build Objection Reframe interaction points into each step of a sales whiteboard, you are arming sellers to answer or deflect objections.

In Part 4 we will look in depth at whiteboard content elements, but generally speaking various whiteboards for sales might include (in no particular order) the following 12 specific actions:

1. Write the whiteboard title.
2. Establish meeting objectives.
3. Confirm the customer's current situation, business objectives, opportunities, and near-term initiatives.
4. Share relevant market trends and typical customer challenges, and capture customer feedback.
5. Share company facts, figures, and other relevant data.
6. Mention third-party validation of your company or solutions (from analysts, publications, media, and other neutral commentators).
7. Render drawings, text, and other visual elements that describe solutions, services, products, and other offerings in a way that demonstrates unique business value.
8. Notate competitive differentiators and silver bullets.
9. Establish "proof points"—case studies and references—where your solutions and services have been successfully delivered with measurable benefits.
10. Summarize the discussion—why should your customer select you?
11. Document next step action items.
12. Capture "parking lot" unanswered questions and follow-up items.

There are no hard and fast rules about the placement or ordering of the above elements on the whiteboard. Not every whiteboard for sales must include all, or even most, of the above ingredients. It all depends on the objective of the whiteboard.

In the following chapters you will see a variety of whiteboard template examples and learn details on how the above ingredients work in different whiteboard types.

Whiteboard Architecture Examples

Let's look at some examples of how to lay out some of the elements on a whiteboard or other drawing surface. You will see the positions of these elements change according to each whiteboard's type, purpose, and sales situation.

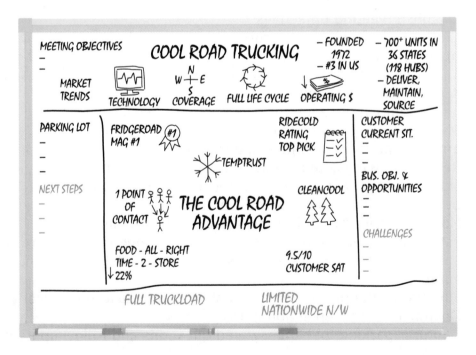

Look at the middle section of the whiteboard on the previous page. The number of ways you can lay out the center of the whiteboard, using visuals, text, and/or schematics, is limitless. You can choose the solution elements, third-party validation, proven success, and competitive weaknesses in whichever ways that will be most effective for a particular sales situation.

Let's look at another potential layout of a whiteboard:

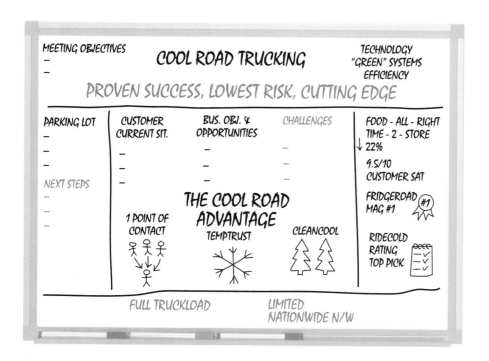

The center part of this whiteboard is different from the last example.

You may have noticed that neither of these example layouts map to the specific whiteboard types we addressed in Chapter 9. The purpose of these whiteboards is simply to demonstrate how various whiteboard ingredients, or content, can be represented in different ways.

In later chapters we'll discuss best practices for how much content a whiteboard for sales should contain, and how to break it into separate steps.

CHAPTER 11

Qualification and Discovery Whiteboards

Through this approach I uncovered opportunities in five different areas of our portfolio. I plan to continue using this approach to discover more opportunities from the Scottish customer base.

—Account Manager, large hardware, software, services company

If you work in a large enterprise, have you ever had presales, technical, or other subject matter expert (SME) resources complain they are being poorly utilized, or being pulled into sales opportunities before the right level of qualification has been done? Salespeople often put the cart before the horse. They use slides and jump to a Solution

Whiteboard before they have confirmed whether or not an opportunity is qualified.

A Qualification and Discovery Whiteboard establishes whether or not—and how—a vendor and prospect should invest time and energy continuing the sales cycle. It's all about taking a prospect's temperature and figuring out whether they are a serious buyer or just kicking tires. These types of whiteboards can be conducted either in person or remotely using distance whiteboarding technology that we explore in detail in Chapter 27. The use of these types of whiteboards usually precedes—and can easily lead to—a Solution Whiteboard, even in the same sales meeting.

Let's look at a number of different Qualification and Discovery Whiteboard frameworks. After you review these examples, take some time to think about other whiteboard structures that may support your own selling style, map to your sales methodology, and align with the type of solutions and services you offer.

The *Four-Quadrant Time and Knowledge Qualification and Discovery Whiteboard*

Ted McCarthy is a professional consulting salesperson based in Austin, Texas. He's one of the most strategic salespeople you will ever meet. Ted designed a Qualification and Discovery Whiteboard that he uses at the beginning of the sales process with a customer. According to Ted, his Four-Quadrant qualification whiteboard has made him "a ton" of money over the course of his career. And the whiteboard doesn't say a single thing about the products or solutions he is selling.

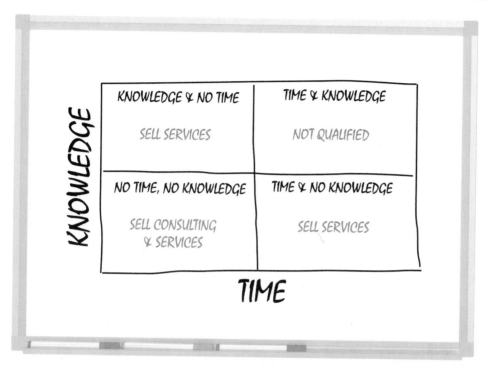

Figure 11.1 **The *Four-Quadrant Time and Knowledge* Qualification and Discovery Whiteboard**

So let's look at a practical way you might use this whiteboard based on Ted's approach. Let's say you are meeting with the CIO of a large contract manufacturing firm. The CIO and her team have been contracted to launch a new product due out by the end of the year. During the meeting you discover that the team knows a lot about the business requirements, tools, and techniques to design and manufacture the product, and they could probably do all the work themselves, but the project deadlines are tight, and the CIO is not sure she can get the work done in time with the resources she has. In this case, the prospect falls into the top left quadrant of the whiteboard: "Knowledge & No Time." What the CIO needs is services.

On the other hand, let's say it's a new type of product that the team doesn't have much experience with, but there is plenty of time to complete the project. In this case, consulting services would be more appropriate.

The other two quadrant scenarios are self-explanatory.

Ted uses this whiteboard at the beginning of all his sales cycles. It achieves four critical objectives:

1. *Positions him as a trusted advisor* who is not just pushing products and services down the throat of his buyer.
2. *Focuses on the buyer's needs*, given their unique sales situation.
3. *Provides a launching point into a more detailed discussion* that may include another Qualification and Discovery Whiteboard, or even a Solution Whiteboard.
4. *Acknowledges it's possible there may not be an opportunity* to do business with the customer if there is not a fit.

The *Don't Waste My Time* Qualification and Discovery Whiteboard

Three out of four of the quadrants in Ted's Qualification and Discovery Whiteboard signal an opportunity to do business with his prospect. Another possible Qualification and Discovery Whiteboard focuses on whether any type of opportunity exists at all. This is the *Don't Waste My Time* Qualification and Discovery Whiteboard.

Most often, this whiteboard is an internal qualification tool that can be used during a phone conversation or following a meeting. It is a diagnostic tool to help you evaluate the quality of a sales lead or opportunity.

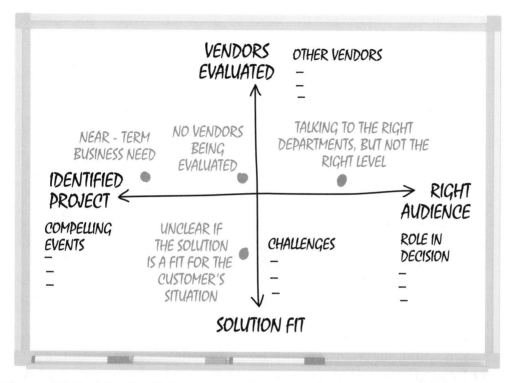

Figure 11.2 The *Don't Waste My Time* Qualification and Discovery Whiteboard

Here is a six-step example of how you could use this whiteboard during a phone conversation.

1. *State that the goal of the meeting* is to find out more about your prospect's current situation and see if there is a fit to do business.
2. *Draw the arrows (without the labels).*
3. *Draw the "Identified Project" label* and ask your prospect if an actual project has been identified or sponsored, or if the interest is purely

information gathering. In the preceding whiteboard, the prospect has communicated there is a near-term business need and compelling event(s).

4. If a project exists, *find out if any other vendors have been or plan to be evaluated.* Knowing whether the prospect is evaluating specific vendors helps you understand if this is a good opportunity to spend time on. In the above example, no other vendors are being evaluated. You may interpret this in two ways. It could indicate the project is not a high priority. Or, you could view it positively as an indication you are either the first vendor being evaluated, or there is an opportunity to create the need for a solution. At the very least, you will be in a position to influence the decision criteria. A follow-up question might be, "Do you plan on evaluating other vendors, and if so, when, and which ones?" On the other hand, if other vendors are being actively evaluated, and your competitors are among them, it is most certainly an opportunity worth pursuing.

5. *Next, is there a solution fit?* It's time to break out your list of qualification questions around typical challenges your solutions can address. If these resonate with your prospect, taken together with positive readings on the other dimensions in the whiteboard, this is a great sign. In the above example, more discovery is required to determine if there is a fit (see the *Are We a Fit?* Qualification and Discovery Whiteboard next).

6. *Are you at the right level?* You could get terrific readings on the first three dimensions only to find you aren't talking with the right person in the organization. In this specific example, you are speaking with someone in the right department, but this person lacks sufficient influence or budget authority to make a purchasing decision.

Based on your particular sales methodology, you can substitute any other labels, dimensions, or concepts into this whiteboard. You can use this template in any order and substitute whichever qualification dimensions you feel are most relevant to your specific selling approach and style. You can interpret the responses you get in a way that maps to your selling style and length of sales cycle.

The *Are We a Fit?* Qualification and Discovery Whiteboard

You can use several Qualification and Discovery whiteboards together. Let's say you get a good reading from the *Don't Waste My Time* Qualification and Discovery Whiteboard, and it is clear that both parties would benefit from a continued dialogue. You can now go to a deeper level using the *Are We a Fit?* Qualification and Discovery Whiteboard to evaluate if the prospect's current situation, goals, and objectives are aligned with your capabilities. While the focus is on your core competencies, there is room to accommodate customer-specific objectives that may or may not be a fit for your offerings.

The following example shows how you would use this Qualification and Discovery Whiteboard in front of a prospect to assess whether they are a good fit. For this example we'll use the Cool Road Trucking case study. The idea is to identify where the prospect believes they are today across a number of core disciplines or current situations, and where they want to be or anticipate being over time, on a scale of 0 to 10. In this way, the prospects are in effect self-qualifying themselves, with a powerful subconscious impact. By the end of the whiteboard, if there is a good fit, it is hard for them to argue that you cannot help them get to where they need to be.

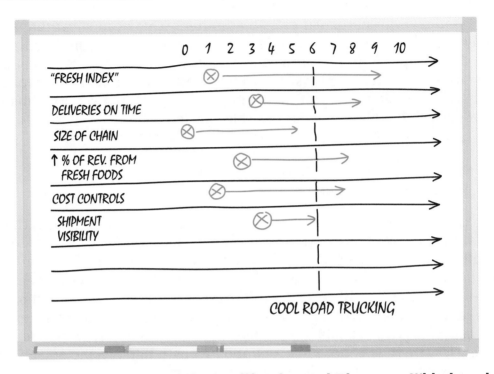

Figure 11.3   The *Are We a Fit?* Qualification and Discovery Whiteboard

This whiteboard is simple to use and most effective with a prospect, whether in person or over web conference with a tablet PC or digital paper. You should use the following six steps:

1. Number the top of the board 0 to 10 from left to right.
2. Draw out the various core competencies enabled by your solutions or services, as depicted, with horizontal right arrows between each. These items could also be qualification criteria that would indicate a good fit, such as "size of chain" or "percent of revenue from fresh foods."
3. Save a couple of rows at the bottom for custom qualification criteria that are specific to each prospect. This is where situational fluency is

ACTIVITY—Develop an *Are We Fit?* Whiteboard for a Current Prospect

Notes

especially valuable to map your solution's capabilities to the unique business needs of your prospect you may not yet be aware of.

4. Working interactively with your prospect, have them assign a value to their *current* situation for each core competency or qualification criterion, working top to bottom. Make sure you capture each current situation value *before* asking them what numeric value they aspire to reach.

5. Next, ask them to assign a value to where they *aspire* to be or *anticipate* being for each criterion, drawing an arrow from the current situation value to the value they assign.

6. Finally, draw a dashed vertical line coming down from the number 6 on the scale. Your solutions and services are designed to bring your prospect "above average" in each of the criteria, at a minimum. Any prospect that wants to be just average is not open to the type of improvement you can offer, or has not yet been convinced they need to change. If you find yourself in this situation, it is a good indication that it is the right time to use one of your handy *Why Change* Whiteboards, which we will discuss in the next chapter.

In the figure above, the specific Cool Road Trucking opportunity is worth further investigation. The prospect is experiencing a high degree of fresh food spoilage; they want to improve delivery times; they are a growing chain, albeit modestly; they anticipate growing the percent of revenue derived from fresh foods; more cost controls are being put in place; and they see room for improvement in shipment visibility. Even though only "fresh index" and "timely deliveries" are above a 7, these are two of the most important indicators of a good Cool Road Trucking opportunity.

Assuming you get positive readings, this whiteboard can create a high degree of buy-in on the part of the prospect to continue through the sales process. The whiteboard is also an excellent tool to help you prioritize your sales activities by focusing on opportunities with the highest readings.

Whichever Qualification and Discovery Whiteboard you choose to use—or perhaps one that you've "home grown"—keep in mind that the purpose is *not* to get into product and solution detail until you know you have a real opportunity. We all love the products and solutions we sell. Holding off on sharing these details can often be the "bait" to reel in your qualified prospect for a second meeting.

ACTIVITIES

Up until now you've been reading, which is a good way for you to learn about whiteboards. But if you are going to really use whiteboards, you have to start trying out what we are talking about. Throughout this section of the book we have Activities. And we literally mean that you should grab a pencil and try them out. Here is the first of these sections.

ACTIVITY

Select an early stage opportunity, or an account that you are prospecting into. Use your available notes or account plan and, using the blank template opposite Figure 11.3, develop an *Are We a Fit?* Qualification and Discovery Whiteboard that you can use with your customer. For now, just supply the qualification criteria or business objectives that define a good fit for your solution or product offering. Later, you can use this whiteboard in front of your prospect to complete it.

In the next chapter we'll look at a possible follow-up to the Qualification and Discovery Whiteboard: Why Change Whiteboards.

CHAPTER 12

Why Change Whiteboards

Sixty-five percent of decision makers will give their business to the company that "builds the buying vision." The other 35 percent said they will conduct a fair-and-square bake-off between the top competitors.

—Forrester Research

Let's take a look at the second whiteboard type, the Why Change Whiteboard. In Chapter 11 we discussed the possibility that a prospect may still be a good candidate for your solution or services, even if on the surface they don't meet all of your baseline qualification criteria, as explored using a Qualification and Discovery Whiteboard. The reality is, they don't know what they don't know.

The Why Change Whiteboard is designed to combat your biggest competitor, which isn't what you think it is. It's not your archrival; in fact, it's a more insidious enemy called "no decision" or "the status quo." According to sales research firm the Sales Benchmark Index, nearly 60 percent of early stage opportunities fall victim to the status quo. These numbers correlate to Forrester's numbers above. If you can't create a buying vision, most prospects will more than likely keep current course and speed, with a minority going the bake-off route and perhaps ending up choosing one of your competitors.

It's a Messaging Problem

Let's look at these numbers more closely. Even if you did decide a prospect is worthy of next steps after using a Qualification and Discovery Whiteboard, a good portion of those prospects you scheduled follow-up meetings with decided they were okay and didn't need to do anything different by the end of the discussion. You *were sure* they were at risk or they might be missing something that is negatively impacting their business. After all, why else would they be willing to meet with you?

So how did you manage to convince someone who was concerned their objectives were at risk that they didn't need your—or anyone else's—solution? More than likely, you came in with your typical "why us" company and product-centric sales messaging too early, and they weren't ready to hear about it. It could have been slides, or even a Solution Whiteboard, used prematurely. The reality is that the majority of the prospects you meet with are still asking themselves, "Why change?" and "Why now?" They live in *their* story, but you insist on telling them *your* story too soon.

Wake Up the Old Brain

Breaking through the status quo is like breaking a habit. Your brain goes on autopilot when a habit is formed. And the part of the brain that makes decisions to change literally goes to sleep. In order to disrupt this habit (the status quo) and reconsider your current approach, you have to wake up this part of the brain where decisions to change are actually made.

It's called the Old Brain (sometimes referred to as the primal brain or lizard brain), designed to ensure your survival. If your Old Brain senses your survival is in jeopardy, or your current situation is unsafe, it causes you to react and move away from the potential threat and seek a "new safe." Your first job is to make sure that your prospect's Old Brain is activated and involved in your presentation, so it's good to know what stimulates the Old Brain.

As a survival mechanism, the Old Brain is more motivated to move away from pain than it is to move toward gain. It is more adaptive and emotional than rational. Whiteboard visuals are a great way to introduce a threat, challenge, problem, potential missed opportunity, or unmet obligation, and create a visceral reaction in your prospect that their desired outcome is at risk.

The Old Brain doesn't have the capacity for language. It performs at a very basic, nearly instinctual level. So the key is to present a scenario that motivates the Old Brain to reconsider its current state. Why Change Whiteboards need to be simple but hard-hitting and show clear contrast—the Old Brain craves contrast to make a distinction. You can't just show your proposed new way of doing things; your approach needs to be presented in the context of why the old way no longer works. Again, whiteboard visuals are a great way to demonstrate clear contrast between why the old is bad and the new is good. The ability of your prospect to perceive value and make a decision lies in this contrast.

Why Change Whiteboards create enough status quo disruption that your prospect has to question their current approach and consider doing something different. If you use it right, this type of whiteboard can help unhinge the incumbent product, service, or process before plunging into your Why Us? Solution Whiteboards, which prematurely elaborate on you, your products, and services.

Let's take a close look at the *Today versus Tomorrow* Why Change Whiteboard using the Cool Road Trucking case study:

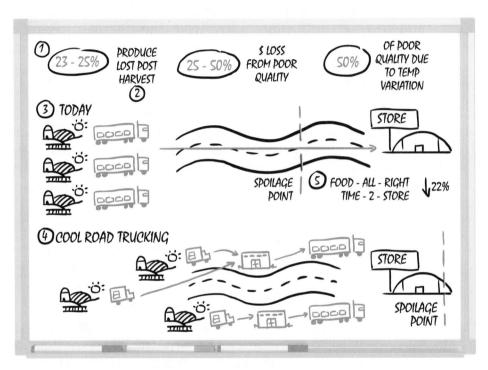

Figure 12.1   The *Today versus Tomorrow* Why Change Whiteboard

You will note that this whiteboard has a series of defined movements designed to provoke the prospect by showing how his or her status quo is unsafe and guide the conversation to your recommended "new safe."

ACTIVITY—Complete a *Today versus Tomorrow* Why Change Whiteboard for a Current Prospect

Notes

1. *It starts with "grabber" statements.* These are typically presented as a series of numbers (in this case, percentages) that have a hidden meaning. Write all the grabbers on the whiteboard *before* revealing their meaning.

2. *The meaning is then unveiled* to introduce an unmet, underappreciated, or even unrealized threat to the status quo. In this case, our grabbers are revealed to be industry average data points on produce spoilage, the significant loss of revenue from poor quality, and that temperature variations account for 50 percent of poor quality.

3. *It then moves to a visual big picture* that paints the prospect's current approach in a painful light. This is presented as a collective understanding of what similar organizations are struggling with based on your company's experience in the market. (Remember, you see more organizations and decision makers who look like your buyer than they do. They expect you to know things they don't and share these insights.) In many cases, food store chains use shipping companies that wait until full truckloads are packed at the source and then driven directly to stores; this causes delays and more temperature variations during transport, leading to rapid spoilage. The dialogue associated with this picture creates an interactive opportunity to determine how similar the prospect's experiences are to the straw man you are presenting. You should then identify the negative business impact created by these "leaks and squeaks" in their status quo. *It is critical* to visually show these gaps or deficits so the decision maker feels the pain.

4. *This creates an urgency to look at possible alternatives.* Once the context for change is established, your whiteboard needs to evolve into a contrasting point of view and begin leading the prospect to your new approach. You must show how these imminent and significant problems can be better solved. The visual should clearly depict a different way of approaching the issues, without going

into a lot of detail on the solution. And your story must focus on those gaps only you can solve, or that you clearly handle in an advantaged way over the status quo. Cool Road Trucking has a "Less-than-Truckload" approach that ships specific produce types faster, centralizing them at temperature-controlled distribution centers and then dispatching them in full truckloads with the latest temperature-controlled technology. The spoilage point is thereby *after* arrival at stores, not in transit.

5. *To close out this whiteboard, you need to share a customer story with contrast.* Your Why Change Whiteboard needs to include at least one story about a customer of yours in the same market that faced a similar challenge and successfully overcame it. This will help your prospects realize they have the same desperate need to change as that company did. Food-All-Right reduced spoilage by 22 percent by doing business with Cool Road.

ACTIVITY

Using the same account you used for one of the Qualification and Discovery Whiteboard activities, or another account that is early in the sales process, complete the *Today versus Tomorrow* Why Change Whiteboard structure using the blank template opposite Figure 12.1.

The Wall Why Change Whiteboard

Let's look at another variant of a Why Change Whiteboard, *The Wall.* The concept is simple: show how a prospect's current situation cannot traverse a set of typical challenges to fully realize opportunities and stated objectives.

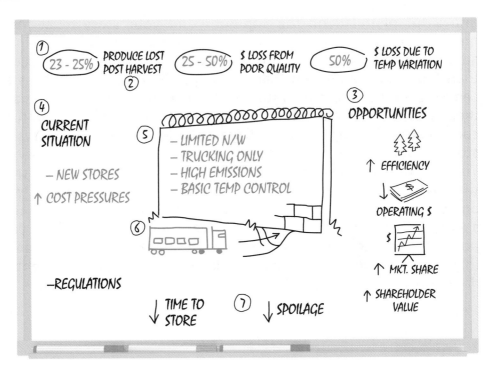

Figure 12.2 *The Wall* **Why Change Whiteboard**

1. This whiteboard also starts with grabbers.
2. The meaning is then unveiled.
3. It then moves to confirming and documenting key opportunities and objectives of the prospect, presented in a way that draws parallels to similar organizations.
4. Document the prospect's current situation.
5. The Wall represents the typical challenges that impact all food stores, preventing them from crossing the chasm from the current situation to the opportunities. As with the previous example, once the context for change is established, your whiteboard needs to evolve into a contrasting point of view.

6. Next, you establish a contrasting approach achieved with your solution. In this case, it's all about how Cool Road can help to break through (or in this case tunnel under) the Wall of Challenges.
7. Finally, you can talk about proof points as you did in the previous example. Here again, you'll notice that the whiteboard completely avoids any in-depth discussion of product or solution detail.

By now, your prospect is hopefully convinced they need to take a different approach—they want to change. But now they'll want to know *how* you will assist them in breaking through the status quo and grasping their opportunities, and why *you* are the best vendor to help them do it. That is achieved using a Solution Whiteboard, examples of which we will introduce in the next chapter.

CHAPTER 13

Solution Whiteboards

Several things make whiteboard selling successful; the approach simplifies complex solutions. The format fosters dynamic group interaction between seller and buyer. PowerPoint is not used. I want you to know this—we use whiteboard selling techniques daily to convey our messages, fill our pipelines, and close business.

—Sales Rep, South Florida

Since 2007—and as of this writing—we have worked with our customers to design and deploy approximately 500 Solution Whiteboards. In some cases, single customers have engaged us to build more than 50 different whiteboards, corresponding to specific products, solutions, or even corporate-level whiteboards that showcase the breadth of solutions that an organization brings to market.

Solution Whiteboards differ from the whiteboards we have showcased so far in a very important way—they talk about the "why you" and "what is it" as opposed to the "why change" and the "why now." They also can follow a Qualification and Discovery Whiteboard designed to discover and learn more about a prospect's challenges and determine whether the opportunity is worthy of further pursuit.

Many Solution Whiteboards are architected to get into a deeper level of detail about the specific components of your solutions and services and the unique value they deliver. From a content perspective, Solution Whiteboards are driven by the information typically contained in traditional sales collateral (slide presentations, datasheets, whitepapers, etc.). Regardless of the level of detail, Solution Whiteboards are sometimes modeled to represent the journey of the customer or a "day in the life."

Solution Whiteboard Examples

In this section we'll showcase several Solution Whiteboards. Remember, you will want to use situational fluency to do the following four things when presenting solution whiteboards:

1. Frequently check in with your customer and ask the right questions at the right time to ensure a two-way information exchange.
2. Pivot based on the prospect's level of interest.
3. Add or omit elements of the whiteboard as necessary.

4. Create a short version of each whiteboard that pulls out information depending on your audience and the amount of time you have to present the story.

One thing you will notice about the Solution Whiteboard examples is that they do not always include all of the whiteboard ingredients we introduced in Chapter 9. You can mix and match the various whiteboard elements as you create your own custom templates tailored to your prospect's unique situation. For example, does your prospect already know the basic facts about your organization? If so, you would probably not want to rehash those in your whiteboard. When it comes to capturing meeting objectives, this is always a good idea, but for the purposes of demonstrating the examples, in some cases there is not enough "real estate" on the pages of this book to include a place for meeting objectives and next steps, which *should* be included in every whiteboard.

The *Level Set Wheel*

The first example is actually a whiteboard that bridges a Qualification and Discovery Whiteboard and a Solution Whiteboard. You can use this whiteboard in a second meeting as a lead-in to a more detailed Solution Whiteboard. Confirming what you've learned in earlier meetings is a *critical* step before you communicate value at a deeper level. The Level Set Wheel will help you do just that—achieve a base level of agreement and establish common ground before getting into any more detail about your solutions or services.

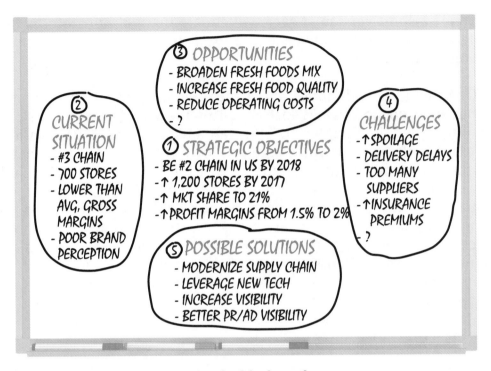

Figure 13.1 **The *Level Set Wheel* Whiteboard**

Let's review each element of the wheel, in the order of how you will draw them. The figure depicts an example of how the Level Set Wheel works when positioning Cool Road Trucking's solutions and services.

Company Strategic Goals and Objectives

Company goals map to your prospect's highest-level business objectives achieved through various initiatives mandated by senior level management and ultimately the CEO and the Board. You will gather this information when doing independent research, during earlier discussions with your prospect, or when using a Qualification and Discovery Whiteboard.

ACTIVITY—Develop a *Level Set Wheel* Whiteboard for a Current Prospect

Notes

Current Situation

The Current Situation maps to your prospect's current environment, investments, existing systems, and processes.

Opportunities

Opportunities represent what is possible in order to position the business to achieve the corporate objectives and initiatives. Opportunities are more specific than the highest-level corporate objectives. They are specific process and task optimizations, cost/risk reducers, or new product offerings.

Challenges

Challenges are the specific business issues and concerns that result from the current situation. Challenges are more specific than current situation elements and are what inhibit or prevent your customer from grasping market opportunities and achieving strategic goals and objectives.

Possible Solutions

Possible solutions are not necessarily the names of your company's specific offerings, but are types of solutions or generic product/solution categories. The idea here is to get the customer to agree they need to do *something*, and are going to select somebody's solution (not necessarily yours) instead of doing nothing and maintaining the status quo. You should not go into any detail about features and functions at this point—just high-level solution categories or possible strategies.

The *Buying Criteria* Solution Whiteboard

The Buying Criteria Whiteboard is a good place to start to demonstrate a very simple Solution Whiteboard. It has a straightforward purpose: show how your organization's solutions can uniquely meet your prospect's key buying criteria. This whiteboard is a way to seed the buying criteria in your favor, something that is often difficult. The secret sauce of this whiteboard is that it leverages a customer example and/or proof point to back up how your solution can meet (or drive the need for) each buying criterion. It also saves room for additional buying criteria that are important to your customer. You will note that the buying criteria should be high level and business value oriented, not feature/function, even though your products' or solutions' key capabilities may be what end up satisfying these buying criteria.

You will also note the use of small, numbered "step bubbles." These serve two functions; one is as a call-out between the whiteboard visual example and the explanation of the purpose of each step, and also to instruct the presenter on the order in which the whiteboard should be drawn.

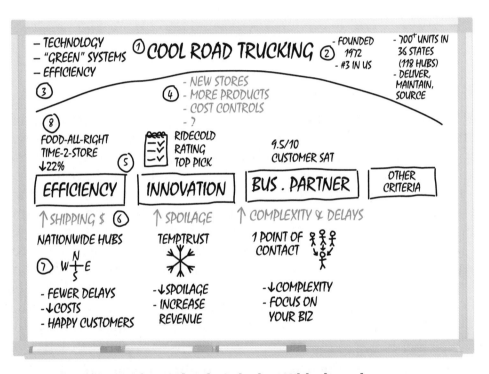

Figure 13.2 **The *Buying Criteria* Solution Whiteboard**

ACTIVITY—Develop a *Buying Criteria* Solution Whiteboard for a Current Prospect

Notes

Let's look at a typical flow of the *Buying Criteria* Solution Whiteboard, in the following eight steps:

1. *The whiteboard title will normally include the product or solution name.* For a higher level Solution Whiteboard it would possibly be your organization's name.
2. *Optionally lead with information about your company.* As mentioned above, this will depend on how much your prospect knows about your company.
3. *Include a discussion of major market trends and themes* to build thought leader and trusted advisor status.
4. *Recap and/or capture key customer challenges.* This shows your prospect you have done your homework.
5. *Introduce key buying criteria that map well to your solution's unique capabilities,* and identify additional buying criteria important to your prospect.
6. *Discuss challenges that drive each buying criteria.* This is needed to establish the importance of each buying criteria you are proposing.
7. *Discuss relevant product and/or solution details and capabilities that map directly to addressing the key buying criteria.* Only pick capabilities that you believe map to your prospect's unique situation and challenges.

8. *Provide references, proof points, and/or other third-party validations that back up your assertions that your solution(s) satisfy each of the buying criteria.*

As mentioned previously, find room for meeting objectives and next steps when presenting this whiteboard.

ACTIVITY

Using the same account you used for the *Level Set Wheel* Whiteboard activity, complete the *Buying Criteria* Whiteboard structure using the blank template opposite Figure 13.2.

The Mountain Solution Whiteboard

The Mountain is an effective Solution Whiteboard template when you are focused on differentiating your solutions or services from those of your competition, and when you want to align your offerings with the journey your customer wants to take based on their business strategy.

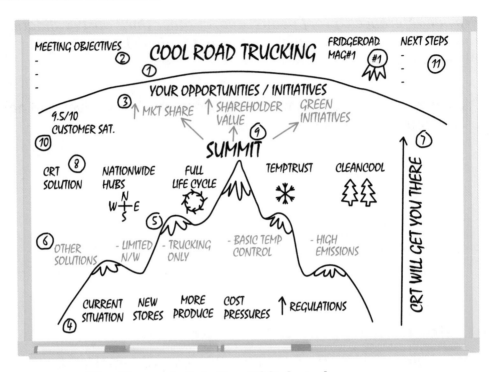

Figure 13.3 *The Mountain* **Solution Whiteboard**

Let's look at the 11 different elements of The Mountain Whiteboard:

1. *The topic of your whiteboard will drive the title.* For a higher level Solution Whiteboard it could be your organization's name, a solution, or use case. A more detailed Solution Whiteboard typically focuses on a product or specific capability.

ACTIVITY—Develop a *Mountain* Solution Whiteboard for a Current Prospect

Notes

2. *Establish the meeting objectives.* These should come from your prospect, but you will also have your own objectives for the meeting.

3. *Where does your customer want to go as a business?* What are their high-level opportunities, business goals, objectives, imperatives, and near-term initiatives? You will have done your homework up front, either on phone calls or through Qualification and Discovery Whiteboards.

4. *Where is your customer's business today?* What are the complications or circumstances blocking them from grasping their business opportunities? This is their current situation.

5. *Draw the mountain*, and talk about how it will be a journey to get from base camp to the summit.

6. *Identify some other competing solutions* your customer has told you they are evaluating that might be misunderstood to offer equivalent capabilities. Identify their limitations that could prevent your prospect from reaching the summit.

7. *Establish you are the only vendor or solution* that can get them to the top of the mountain.

8. *Identify the unique elements of your solution* that deliver business value and that your competitors lack.

9. *If necessary, further explain how you can help your prospect reach the summit* and grasp the opportunities identified at the beginning of the dialogue.

10. *Provide one additional proof point or case study.*
11. *Capture next steps and identify action items.*

ACTIVITY

Using the same account you used for the "Level Set Wheel" whiteboard activity, complete *The Mountain* Whiteboard structure using the blank template opposite Figure 13.3.

The *Day-in-the-Life* Solution Whiteboard

The Day-in-the-Life Whiteboard enables you to delve a little bit deeper into a specific solution or product. It also provides an opportunity to showcase the unique capabilities you offer to address real-world customer challenges. You do this by tracking an individual within your prospect's organization, someone who is struggling with their current situation throughout the day. This whiteboard is especially effective in fostering interaction between you and your prospect. It meets the key requirement of positioning you as a thought leader, and will help you confirm your prospect's existing situation.

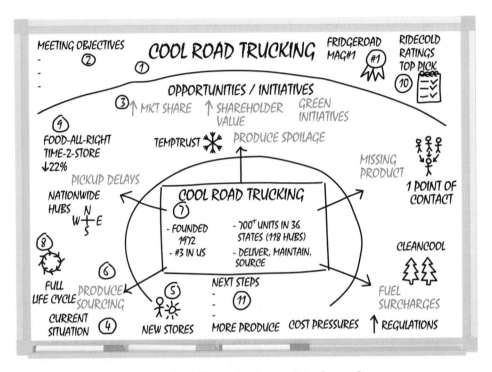

Figure 13.4   The *Day-in-the-Life* Solution Whiteboard

Some Solution Whiteboards spend less time reviewing typical trends and challenges. Instead, you will focus more on specific customer issues and how discrete solution elements address them using a story framework. The *Day-in-the-Life* Solution Whiteboard does this through the following 10 steps.

1. *The topic of your whiteboard* will normally be related to a specific solution or product.

ACTIVITY—Complete a *Day-in-the-Life* Solution Whiteboard for a Current Prospect

Notes

2. *Establish the meeting objectives.* These should come from your prospect but you will also have your own objectives for the meeting. Also make it clear you will be asking for concrete next steps at the end of the meeting.

3. *Recap what you know about your prospect's high-level opportunities*, business goals, objectives, imperatives, and near-term initiatives.

4. *Confirm through discussion and interaction the current business situation of your customer.*

5. *Position the Day-in-the-Life as a way to track typical challenges throughout a hypothetical day*, draw the circle from rise and shine to going to the pub after a long day. The "day" is a condensed metaphor for the general business situation your prospect is in.

6. *Move around the circle and introduce some typical challenges*, asking, "Does this happen to you" or "Have you had this problem," or "In our earlier discussions you mentioned you had challenges with. . . ." Using situational fluency you can add challenges that you were not previously aware of.

7. *Position your company* as the only vendor that can "save the day." Do not go into solution detail yet.

8. *Follow the same path around the circle as you knock off each of the challenges* by describing the unique capabilities of your solution and how they address the previously identified challenges.

9. *Intersperse examples of how you have delivered similar benefits* for existing customers as you discuss how your solution addresses the prospect's challenges.

10. *Revisit Next Steps to identify action items.*

ACTIVITY

Using the same account you used for the previous whiteboard activities, complete the *Day-in-the-Life* Whiteboard structure using the blank template opposite Figure 13.4. Here again, observe how some Solution Whiteboard elements are present while others are not, and how their order is changed.

CHAPTER 14

Competitive Whiteboards

I hope [biggest competitor] does not find out about this until I sell our solutions to all of Texas. What a great secret weapon we have stumbled upon.

—New Hire Sales Rep, South Florida

There are two ways that whiteboarding is *the* competitive weapon: (1) The very fact that you are using a whiteboard, and not Power-Point, will set you apart from your slide jockey competitors. But more importantly, (2) when you are whiteboarding your solution in front of your prospect, you can visually show the unique advantage your solution delivers compared to your competitors'. You can plant land mines or use silver bullets to de-fang your competition.

In this chapter we will explore several examples of whiteboard structures that deliver that knockout blow by making your unique differentiators crystal clear in a head-to-head comparison.

Bash or Be Bashed

When we work with our clients, we often hear, "We don't want to mention our competition by name in our whiteboards, it's not our style." For the most part we agree. It's often better presentation etiquette to refer to competitors obliquely by saying "the other guys," or "the leading vendor," or "the incumbent vendor." That way you don't appear to be bashing your competition.

However, there are many situations where the prospect will explicitly ask you how you stack up against a particular vendor, either because they are conducting a head-to-head evaluation for a new project, or because they are considering replacing their existing provider. Some salespeople take a more aggressive sales approach. They know their competitor is mounting a frontal assault and they want to meet them head-on.

A Note about Competitive Differentiators

You can choose from the competitive whiteboard templates described below based on your unique selling situation. But before you choose a template, you should first consider which and what kind of differentiators you will highlight in the whiteboard discussion. Part 4 goes into detail on this topic, so please refer to it before building out your competitive whiteboards.

Competitive Whiteboard Examples

There are two main types of Competitive Whiteboards:

1. *Competitive Retrofit*—These whiteboards simply add competitive visual elements to an existing whiteboard. Let's say you begin a meeting with your prospect using a Solution Whiteboard that does not include competitive information, but the prospect explicitly asks for a comparison. Or you learn through the discussion that another vendor is being strongly considered. You can make slight structural modifications and add visual elements within the framework of the original whiteboard. You might remove a component or make some layout and flow changes, but the overall look and feel of the original whiteboard stay the same.
2. *Competitive Whiteboards*—This is a whiteboard you design from the ground up to "go for the throat" and provide a direct comparison to a competing vendor.

Let's take a detailed look at some examples of these two types.

Example #1: Competitive Retrofit—The Buying Criteria Whiteboard

Let's look at an example of how we can take an existing Solution Whiteboard—The Buying Criteria Whiteboard—and add a very simple competitive element to it. The figure below shows how we have added space at the bottom to indicate that a particular competing vendor lacks your capability linked to each buying criteria. We also removed the "Problem Addressed" section, although if you have more space on the whiteboard or other drawing surface, feel free to leave that in.

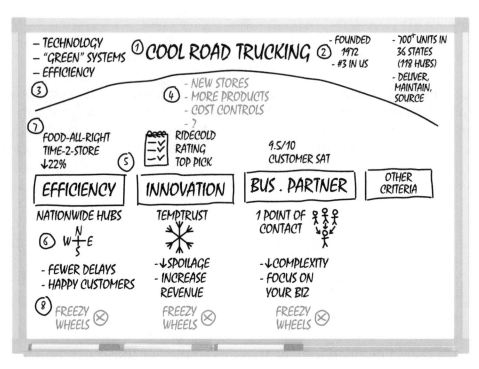

Figure 14.1 *Competitive Retrofit—The Buying Criteria* **Whiteboard**

ACTIVITY

Revisit the *Buying Criteria* Solution Whiteboard example you prepared in Chapter 13, pick your biggest competitor, and, using the blank template opposite Figure 14.1, add the competitive knocks or deficiencies at the bottom of the whiteboard.

Example #2: Competitive Retrofit—The Buying Criteria Whiteboard (Home Remodel)

The next example uses the same basic structure as the Buying Criteria Whiteboard, but it goes a step further in the retrofit by adding a detailed competitive comparison column and more unique solution capabilities.

ACTIVITY—Revisit the *Buying Criteria* Solution Whiteboard to Include Competitive Elements

Notes

The focus is still on the three buying criteria where you hold the largest competitive advantage over the competitor or group of competitors. The result looks like the figure below.

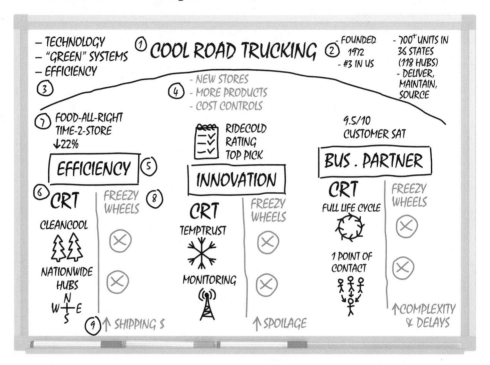

Figure 14.2 *Competitive Retrofit—The Buying Criteria* **Whiteboard (Home Remodel)**

Here are three important things to consider about this whiteboard:

1. It slightly "up-levels" the conversation toward the end by focusing in on the business risk that would result if your prospect were to select your competitor.
2. It adds room for more features and benefits for the purposes of the head-to-head comparison.
3. It still relies on customer proof and references to demonstrate the importance of the buying criteria and key capabilities.

ACTIVITY—Revisit the *Buying Criteria* Solution Whiteboard to Include a Detailed Competitive Comparison

Notes

Example #3: The Four-Quadrant Typical Approach Whiteboard

Let's look at a whiteboard designed from the ground up to showcase your advantages over your competitors. In this case, we avoid a frontal assault and go with a softer "typical approaches" angle. The term "typical approaches" is an oblique reference to competing vendors.

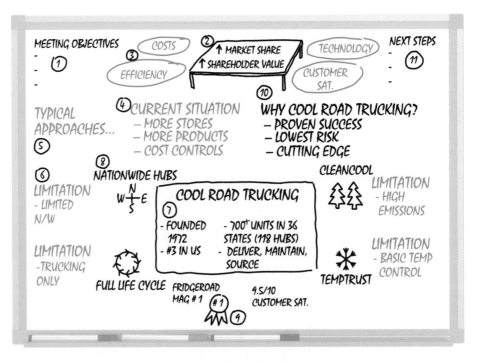

Figure 14.3 The *Four-Quadrant Typical Approach* Whiteboard

ACTIVITY—Complete a *Four-Quadrant Typical Approach* Whiteboard Using a Current Prospect

Notes

The vendors aren't explicitly named, but they are still relegated to the dustbin of old and tired approaches. Or you can replace "typical approaches" with a specific competitor name if you want to be explicit. "Typical approaches" could also refer to the status quo of making "no decision" and sticking with the current, broken approach.

Let's walk through the 11 steps of this whiteboard so that you can understand how it is constructed.

1. *Open with meeting objectives.* You can add a case study or reference to pique the interest of your audience.
2. *If necessary, confirm or discover* business objectives, market opportunities, and near-term initiatives.
3. *If necessary, share typical trends and challenges*, and qualify.
4. *Confirm prospect's current situation* (existing business, broken business process, limitations). Challenges shared or discovered in #3 above can be documented here. This section may not be necessary.
5. *Write "Typical Approaches" or competitor name.*
6. *List limitations with the typical or competitive approach*, moving clockwise from the upper left. Tie back each limitation to the prospect's current situation and the trends and challenges above. This is effective because it clarifies how these limitations are meaningful to the prospect and represent business risk.
7. *If necessary, speak briefly about your organization and key solution areas.* This may include key facts and data points or a list of the various solution categories you provide. Basic information about your organization doesn't always have to be discussed at the beginning of the whiteboard discussion. In fact, these details often have more impact once you have earned the right to proceed through the discussion by establishing trusted advisor and thought leadership status earlier in the knowledge exchange.

8. *Identify key solution capabilities* and explain how they directly address each of the limitations of the typical or competing approaches. Tie back each capability to how your solution and its unique capabilities address the prospect's current situation, and how you will be able to uniquely help them meet their business objectives, grasp market opportunities, and complete their near-term initiatives.

9. *Highlight a relevant case study or proof point* as you discuss unique capabilities in each quadrant, preferably with measurable benefits.

10. *Summarize with why your solution is superior* to typical or competing approaches. By the way, this "Why us" section is a whiteboard component you can use in any whiteboard story.

11. *Close* with actionable next steps.

The above sequencing is very effective. There are also three alternate flows you can use with this whiteboard. You could:

1. Introduce your solution and all four quadrants of your key capabilities before talking about the typical approaches and limitations.

2. Introduce your key capabilities after each set of typical approach limitations.

3. Avoid the discussion of the prospect's current situation altogether, and instead address typical approach limitations and your key capabilities in whatever sequence makes sense.

When it comes to whiteboarding, you have ultimate flexibility in structure, flow, content, interaction, and all other ingredients. That rule does not change with respect to competitive whiteboards. Our goal is to get you thinking about how to structure any whiteboard story and dialogue.

Example #4—The Cost/Risk to Value Whiteboard

Let's look at an example of a strategic-minded whiteboard that positions your company and solutions as more innovative and cutting edge.

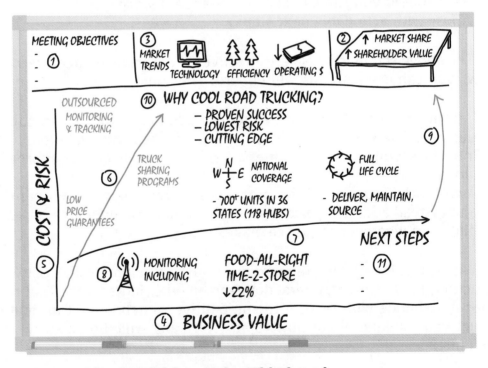

Figure 14.4 **The *Cost/Risk to Value* Whiteboard**

ACTIVITY—Complete a *Cost/Risk to Value* Whiteboard Using a Current Prospect

Notes

This whiteboard shows your customer how they can achieve their business goals and seize market opportunities at much lower cost and risk than your competition. This is an especially effective whiteboard framework if you are competing against a vendor with a lower initial price point. Your objective is to show how the lower "teaser rate" is chicanery, and how the cost and risk to your prospect will grow dramatically without commensurate business value if they choose your competition.

Let's look at the 11 steps of this whiteboard's flow:

1. *Open with meeting objectives.* You can add a case study or reference to pique the interest of your audience.
2. *If necessary, confirm and discover* business objectives, market opportunities, and near-term initiatives.
3. *If necessary, share typical trends and challenges,* and qualify.
4. *Draw* "Business Value" on the X axis.
5. *Draw* "Cost/Risk" on the Y axis.
6. *Draw the vertical red line.* Although the competition may have a lower initial price, total cost of ownership (TCO) and overall business risk increase rapidly and result in limited business value. Make sure the points along this line specifically address the competitor's solution, product, or pricing gimmicks/limitations that support this argument.
7. *Draw the arc* representing your solution's lower longer term cost to deliver meaningful business value, and lower risk to implement, install, or deploy.
8. *Specifically identify solution capabilities* that support this assertion, backed up by customer case studies that demonstrate measurable business value related to that topic. Notice that you can position various elements of your solution or overall offerings as delivering increasing business value at modestly increasing cost. This is especially relevant if you have multiple versions of your solutions or

products with increasing functionality, or add-ons to provide cross-sell and up-sell opportunities. Your objective is to position you as the vendor offering the most complete, low-risk, and advanced solution on the market.

9. *Draw a line from the end of your solution arc* up to the table with the business objectives to highlight that only you can get your prospect where they need to be; your competition will fall far short.

10. *Summarize with why your solution is superior* to typical approaches or a specific competitor's approach.

11. *Close* with actionable next steps.

Competitive whiteboards can be effective competitive weapons, but use them selectively and only if your prospect has agreed to—or better yet, asked to—have such a discussion.

ACTIVITY

Pick your biggest competitor and, using the blank template opposite Figure 14.3, build the *Cost & Risk to Value* Whiteboard per the above structure and flow. Pick one of your largest target accounts and model the whiteboard design to align with their key business objectives and market opportunities, and show how you can get them there faster and at lower cost.

CHAPTER 15

Business Case Whiteboards

Not everything that can be counted counts and not everything that counts can be counted.

—Albert Einstein

As it relates to sales, Einstein's quote is instructive in two ways:

1. If you want to use metrics or key performance indicators (KPIs) as part of making a business case for your products or services, they had better be ones that matter to your prospects and that are highly relevant to their strategic goals and objectives.

2. Business value derived from a product or service cannot be measured solely in a qualitative fashion; quantitative benefits are also important considerations.

When it comes to the quantitative counting, at some point in the sales process (usually in the later stages), your prospect will need to justify the purchase of your product, solution, or service to the bean counters, who may include the CFO, controller, or other members of upper management who control the purse strings. In many cases, providing this data is merely a formality; your buyer needs to check a box that you have provided some sort of ROI or TCO (total cost of ownership) data to back up the decision. This is just more ammunition your champion needs when freeing up budgets controlled by others.

As it relates to our fictional prospect—Foody's Fresh Foods—we know their upper management and Board of Directors have a number of strategic goals and objectives. The key is to count the value of Cool Road Trucking's benefits in a way that maps directly to these objectives. Foody's wants to increase net margin from 1.5 percent to 2 percent, and they see margin increases in fresh foods (produce, meat, fish, etc.) as a way to get there. And increasing shareholder value is predominantly a result of bottom line revenue increase. So when it comes to putting together a business case, these are two KPIs that are natural first candidates.

Putting together a business case is most often done using spreadsheets or ROI calculators. In fact, entire companies have been built to provide web-based ROI tools that enable the buyer to simply go online and input their own data to make a business case without the salesperson's involvement. We believe, however, that this couldn't be more antithetical to the philosophies of customer intimacy and knowledge ownership embodied by whiteboard selling. "Disintermediating" the seller is the last thing you want to do when trying to foster a bond with your prospect. If you are going to present a business case, do it *in person*, and with full knowledge ownership (or in this case "data ownership"). Remember, one function of trusted advisor status is that you have taken the time to learn your prospect's business and have complete knowledge of the key metrics that will drive their success. Your first reaction may be, "How am I going to memorize all of the numbers and metrics in this kind of whiteboard?" In the next section of this book, we will provide some proven strategies on how to quickly memorize *any* whiteboard content, and master the whiteboard in less than two hours—*guaranteed*!

In fact, we contend that the content of a Business Case Whiteboard is secondary to the impact of your capability as a salesperson and the message it sends to your prospect about the lengths to which you will go to understand their business and earn their trust and confidence.

In the following Business Case Whiteboard example, we have modeled how *just two* of Cool Road Trucking's unique capabilities will directly drive two of Foody's KPIs—net margins and bottom line revenue. Let's take a close look at each component of this Business Case Whiteboard, how it flows, and why it is effective.

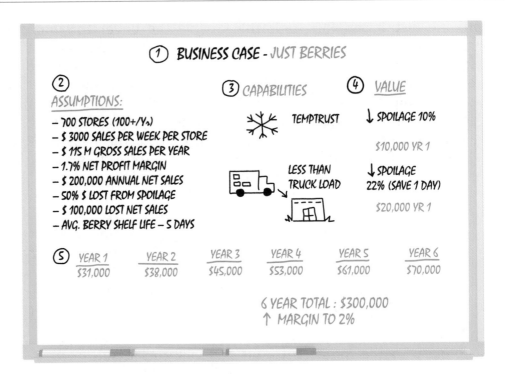

Figure 15.1 *Business Case* **Whiteboard Example**

1. *The title of the whiteboard should include "Business Case" and the part of the business or KPI you are focusing on.* In this case we are only focusing on how Cool Road Trucking will benefit the sales and net margin of berries, just one of dozens of fresh food categories. By focusing in on *just one* of many fresh food categories, we achieve two things; first, we can potentially justify a switch to Cool Road by savings and benefit in one category alone; and second, we select a manageable amount of data that can be mastered in a single whiteboard. More comprehensive ROI and TCO data for other fresh food categories can be provided in a spreadsheet or other tool as a follow-up. Remember, the point of a Business Case Whiteboard is "shock and awe," not boiling the oceans of data.

ACTIVITY—Complete a *Business Case* Whiteboard Using a Current Prospect's Information

Notes

2. *The next part of the whiteboard are the assumptions of the business case.* It is absolutely critical that you lay out data points and other metrics that you and your prospect 100 percent agree on. In this case, much of this is straight math driven by two key metrics: number of planned store openings and average sales of berries per week per store, both data points supplied by Foody's. The other data is simply math derived from these metrics, as well as industry-accepted figures related to spoilage rates and product shelf life. When using industry data, you will need to provide substantiated sources of this information and get agreement from your customer that these metrics are accurate and acceptable for use in the business case. *It is critical* that you secure agreement from your prospect (either through e-mail or a phone call) that your business case assumptions are agreeable *before* you show up to deliver your Business Case Whiteboard. Otherwise you will go down a rat hole debating the accuracy of the assumptions before you get into the really valuable part of the discussion—the measurable benefits of your offerings.

3. *Key capabilities.* Select no more than two or three unique capabilities that deliver measurable value relative to your prospect's key performance indicators. In this case Cool Road is focusing on reducing spoilage in order to both increase revenue and increase net margins.

4. *Value delivered.* This is one of the most debatable parts of the business case, because it assumes that your prospect buys into your claims that your solution "reduces x by y" or "increases a by b" and so on. It is important to have well-substantiated data points to back up your claims of savings or other gains derived by specific capabilities. In the hypothetical business case, Cool Road engaged an independent research firm to measure spoilage rate reductions tied to the TempTrust system installed on all of its refrigerated trucking systems. TempTrust is designed to evenly distribute cooling through the container to reduce spoilage of different food types. The findings were documented in a published study that was picked up and

featured by *FridgeRoad* magazine, which lends credibility to the data points. The second capability, Less-Than-Truck-Load, allows smaller refrigerated trucks to pick up specific types of goods and deliver them to central distribution facilities faster for expedited delivery to stores, instead of sitting on pallets awaiting larger trucks to be filled. The data point of 22 percent reduced spoilage was backed up by a documented case study of another Cool Road Trucking customer, Food-All-Right, which substantiated this benefit in a reference story.

5. *Projected savings.* The final part of a Business Case Whiteboard is simply projecting spoilage savings (and thus increased revenue) based on Foody's store growth plans. Probably the most impactful metric is that when you reduce the $100k lost net annual revenue of berries due to spoilage by the annual reduction in spoilage delivered by Cool Road Trucking systems, Foody's can increase net margins on berries to 2 percent, which exactly matches their stated business objective.

The most frequently heard objection to putting together a Business Case Whiteboard is that many sellers simply lack solid metrics and proven ROI/TCO data for their products or services. We can't really help in this category, other than suggest you work with your existing customers to come up with any type of measurable benefits you can leverage. Remember, the real value of a Business Case Whiteboard is not so much in the content, it's in the fact that you *took the time* to put it together, memorize it, and have the wherewithal to present it to your customer *without* the use of a spreadsheet or other tool.

ACTIVITY

Using an account in the later stages of the sales process, complete a *Business Case* Whiteboard using the blank template opposite Figure 15.1.

CHAPTER 16

Closing Whiteboards

Because only one thing counts in this life: GET THEM TO SIGN ON THE LINE WHICH IS DOTTED.... Money's out there. You pick it up, it's yours. You don't, I got no sympathy for you. You wanna go out on those sits tonight and close, CLOSE. It's yours. If not you're gonna be shining my shoes.

—Blake (Alec Baldwin), *Glengarry Glen Ross*, 1992

A–B–C. A for always, B for be, C for closing; always be closing— *always* be closing. Those famous lines reverberate through the heads of many a salesperson whose manager has sent them the video of that famous scene for which Alec Baldwin was Oscar-nominated. The point of sharing the quote is not that a Closing Whiteboard must *always* be used, or that it should be used as a hammer. It is simply a reminder that there comes a point in the sales process where you have to bring closure and ask for the business.

The Closing Whiteboard is often used in front of the ultimate economic decision maker, and it's designed to encapsulate the most salient points of previously delivered whiteboards used with lower-level champions or influencers. Necessary due diligence (reference checking, etc.), competitive differentiation in your favor, and preliminary financial negotiations should have already occurred prior to using this whiteboard. It's also important to note that this whiteboard may not be necessary, especially if you have been selling to the economic buyer during earlier stages in the sales process.

There are many approaches to closing a sales opportunity, none of which we especially espouse in the context of a Closing Whiteboard. Here are three of them.

1. The Assumptive Close:
   (a) "I wonder what your competition will think when they hear about this."
   (b) "Would you want us to handle sourcing as well as refrigerated trucking?"
   (c) "When do you want the contract effective date?"
2. The Alternative Close:
   (a) "Would you prefer trucks with just TempTrust or also CleanCool?"
   (b) "Shall we meet with your CIO this week or next to get sign off?"
   (c) "Which of your existing suppliers should we start to work with?"

3. The Trial Close:
   (a) "Do you like what I've shared with you so far?"
   (b) "Does this sound good to you?"
   (c) "We offer a pretty compelling solution, wouldn't you agree?"
   (d) "Have I missed anything that is important to your decision?"

Within the context of a consultative sale—especially when selling "enterprise class" solutions—these techniques may not prove effective. You will position yourself well to close by simply laying out the facts of your prospect's current situation, reiterating the consensus around information already provided, and solidifying your trusted advisor status through use of visuals and intimate knowledge of your prospect's business. Naturally, you can use any sales methodology or closing model you have found to be effective, but erring on the side of facts and consensus built so far using other whiteboards is fundamental to a whiteboard selling approach to closing a sale.

A good Closing Whiteboard is simply an amalgamation of several whiteboard types we have previously reviewed: Why Change Whiteboards, Solution Whiteboards, Competitive Whiteboards, and probably most important, a Business Case Whiteboard. They typically contain less information and follow the "Why Change," "Why Now," and "Why Us" model. Let's take a look at an example of a Closing Whiteboard, the *Why Change, Why Now, Why Us* Whiteboard. Each component of this whiteboard plays an important role in setting up the close.

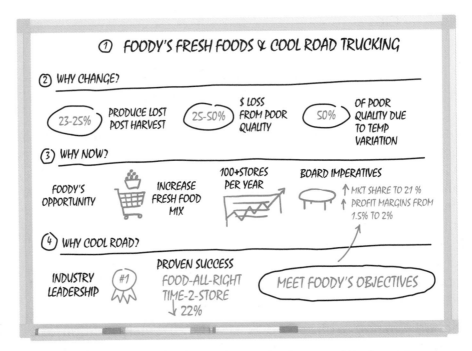

Figure 16.1 The *Why Change, Why Now, Why Us* Whiteboard

1. *The title of the whiteboard* should always start with the prospect's name plus your organization's name. Putting the prospect's name first puts the focus on them and the benefits they will derive as a result of partnering with you.

2. *The Why Change section* is borrowed verbatim from the Why Change Whiteboard; it is important for the economic buyer to see neutral facts about the current situation in the marketplace. A Cool Road Trucking salesperson would probably use the lost revenue in the Berries category here as well, to provide the economic buyer with an example of the lost opportunity cost. Aversion to pain is a major consideration here.

3. *The Why Now section* focuses on Foody's immediate needs and opportunities, based on changes in their business model, as well as

ACTIVITY—Complete a *Why Change, Why Now, Why Us* Whiteboard Using a Current Prospect

Notes

their strategic goals and objectives. It is an opportunity to remind the economic buyer about current, pressing business imperatives that must be met. So what has happened so far? You have told the Foody's economic buyer they are not alone, you have established the reality of lost revenue opportunity (Why Change), and then linked this to Foody's pressing strategic objectives and current situation (Why Now).

4. *The Why Us section* is the bow that wraps everything up by positioning Cool Road Trucking as the only solution that can help Foody's change now to achieve their strategic objectives. Establishing market leadership and proven success here are paramount. You can also reference due diligence completed by your champions and influencers at lower levels in the organization, to substantiate metrics such as increasing margin. If required, you may need to pull out your Business Case Whiteboard to resubstantiate your claims around measurable benefit.

You may be wondering, how would you conclude this whiteboard with a closing statement? You might try something like this:

Working with your team we have established a business case that demonstrates how Foody's and Cool Road Trucking can partner to deliver unique and measurable business value to positively impact the bottom line and help meet your strategic objectives starting today. We would like to earn your business and ask that you consider our proposal for approval today so we can begin achieving these benefits in the very near term.

ACTIVITY

Using an account in the later stages of the sales process, complete a *Why Change*, *Why Now*, *Why Us* Closing Whiteboard using the blank template opposite Figure 16.1.

Another example of a Closing Whiteboard summarizes the key stakeholders who have been met with, and a summary of the sales process to date. This approach is effective because it demonstrates to the economic buyer(s) that you have cast a broad net within the organization, making sure to communicate to all the key players how your solution addresses their specific needs and desires. The whiteboard identifies some key capabilities, but notice how it doesn't refer to specific feature names. The focus is on Next Steps to motivate action.

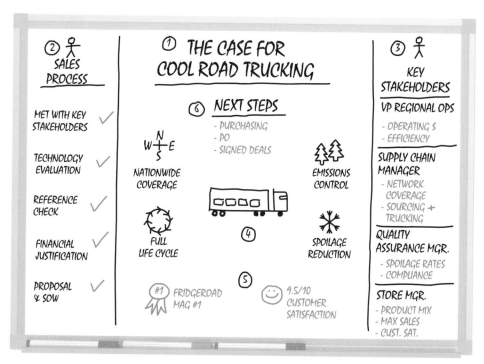

Figure 16.2 *Closing* **Whiteboard Example #2**

We've shared quite a few whiteboard template examples. In Part 4 we will dive into what it will take to leverage one of these templates to build a whiteboard using the whiteboard selling methodology and design best practices.

PART 4

Building a Whiteboard for Sales

CHAPTER 17

Are You Ready to Whiteboard? Not So Fast!

A pressing challenge for a large enterprise is getting sales, marketing, training, and other content developers on the same page when designing effective sales tools used at the point of sale. In my experience running marketing teams at large enterprises and in start-ups, collaborating to build visual stories—aka whiteboards—*is a rallying cry to bring x-functional teams together to gain consensus on messaging and how it should be communicated. Whiteboard selling is not just an outstanding way to communicate value to customers and prospects—it helps organizations come together to provide tools that salespeople actually use, thus ensuring the message gets out in a consistent fashion.*

—Brian Bell, Chief Marketing Officer, Zuora

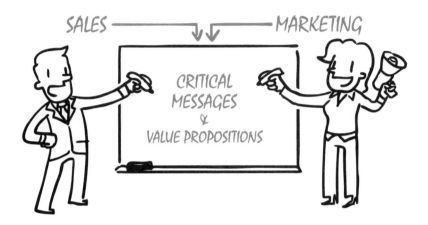

After all the whiteboard examples we've shared and the activities we hope you've completed, you may say to yourself, "I've got some great whiteboard templates built out, now I'm going to go out and start whiteboarding with my customers." Feel free to try out some ideas, but if you're serious about creating sales culture change, there's a long road ahead before rolling out whiteboards to your sales force.

Depending on your role, here are some guidelines on next steps.

Individual Sales Contributors

First, make sure you have completed some of the activities in the previous section in order to create customized examples of some of the whiteboard templates. Model the examples with a specific customer or prospect in mind, perhaps an account you are trying to penetrate or close a deal with right now. In later sections we'll discuss some best practices for how to learn to present a completed whiteboard for sales. Feel free to jump ahead if you are anxious to try out your whiteboard ideas. But before you engage with prospects directly using these new sales tools, be sure to test them out with your colleagues or existing customers to get their feedback and input.

   A *note of caution:* If you find your whiteboards are effective and you decide to document and distribute them in scanned drawings or photos, you must realize you are at risk of running afoul of marketing teams and executives who have not put their stamp of approval on the core messaging contained in your pitch. The market trends, typical challenges, value propositions, competitive information, case studies, and other whiteboard ingredients may not reflect corporate-sanctioned doctrine. Just as home-grown PowerPoint presentations may raise the ire of the message owners, a "skunkworks" whiteboard—if widely distributed—can result in "blowback."

Marketing Managers and Executives

If your objective is to create highly effective whiteboarding tools to arm your sales force on a large scale, your work has just begun. In this book you've seen several highly effective templates and story designs, but a whiteboard design effort usually results in a one-of-a-kind piece of art that uniquely meets the needs of the sales channel. You want to free your salespeople from the evil clutches (and crutches) of PowerPoint. But your success will depend on a high degree of collaboration, working with a x-functional team. You may need to free up resources that are currently tasked with everyday marketing functions in order to make your unique whiteboards come to life.

Sales Enablement Teams

You sit at the crosshairs of sales, marketing, training, products, HR, and many other groups within modern-day companies. We've seen white-boarding initiatives be *the* most strategic endeavors an enablement group undertakes. We've seen whiteboards create tremendous value across the organization and bridge the gap between marketing and sales. As with your marketing counterparts, however, you'll need to put together a x-functional team to get buy-in from all the key players.

Sales Leaders and Executives

When it comes to sales transformation, a whiteboarding initiative is just one piece of the puzzle. Your key role to make this successful comes down to one word: leadership. *Every* successful whiteboarding initiative we've witnessed relies on sales executives to lead and drive the project. You have to ensure complete participation by all groups and create a sense of accountability that drives all the way down to each field person's responsibility to learn and master the story. If you are going to truly enable your sales team to whiteboard your story effectively, you have to *certify* that each and every seller can articulate the story in a high-pressure, simulated sales call. This process will be a topic of a later chapter.

Leadership to make a whiteboarding initiative successful also means you have to allocate a good chunk of time at upcoming sales kickoffs and other meetings to run hands-on whiteboard training. You want to be sure your entire field organization can master the story and go out the very next day and engage with customers and prospects. We've worked with sales organizations large and small that build their entire sales kickoff or other sales event around whiteboard learning and training. They have a strategic view of using whiteboards to enable their sales teams to be more effective.

Preparing for Your Whiteboarding Initiative

We don't use the word "initiative" lightly. Rolling out whiteboarding is not just a "one and done" proposition. We've seen organizations that deploy one whiteboard and soon find themselves in the midst of a full-blown program to roll out whiteboard stories for all of their major solution sets and new product launches. If you want to ensure that the stories are repeatable and adopted, then you have to plan and get broad participation. This is a truly *programmatic* initiative. And even if you've got our whiteboard creation best practices under your belt, short-circuiting the step-by-step design process can result in a final deliverable that misses the mark.

There are three key steps required to lay the groundwork for the whiteboard design process:

1. *Agree on a whiteboard topic.* Before you begin the project, you will most likely have some candidate topics for the first whiteboard you want to build and deploy for sales. After all, there is a reason you have read this far! But there are lots of scope questions that need answering before you choose which whiteboard(s) to create first. Of all the different whiteboard stories you want to deploy to sales, where will you start? What is the right level of the discussion? Who is the target audience? Who will be delivering it? The answers to these questions are driven by the higher-level business and sales objectives of your organization.

2. *Forming a working team.* This is one of the most important and critical success factors of the entire initiative. The right people on the working team will make or break your effort to roll out an effective whiteboard for sales. The whiteboard objectives and scope defined in number 1 above will determine who the key stakeholders are that need to be part of the team. Other important considerations include the size of the working team and the roles of the members.

3. *Take a message inventory.* This is usually not an exercise in creating messaging. Messaging already exists—in the many different Power-Point presentations, Word documents, sales tools, website content, and other sources. Now the working team has to identify which

messaging should be included in the whiteboard story, and make sure that all the various whiteboard ingredients are thrown into the mix.

We have devoted Chapters 18, 19, and 20 to each of these critical steps to ensure that you properly lay the groundwork before you even begin to design your whiteboard.

CHAPTER 18

Choosing the Right Topic for Your Whiteboard

If your objective is to embark on a serious whiteboard design project, you will no doubt have already put some thought into what your objectives are for the whiteboard. You probably have finite resources, and you probably want to respect the time and effort of your working team, once it is formed. So you need to think carefully about the topic you choose for the whiteboard. The topic will then drive the type and scope of the whiteboard, tell you who should be on the working team, determine the materials and key whiteboard ingredients you'll need, and define the project timeline.

Selecting a Whiteboard Topic

A PowerPoint presentation can be built rapidly, in a vacuum, and distributed to sales to be used tactically. A whiteboard is the basis for a well-conceived campaign that touches a x-functional group and has high visibility. What might seem like an obvious first candidate whiteboard topic may not be aligned with the needs of the sales force. When considering the topic and objectives of your whiteboard, you should test your assumptions by asking and answering these 10 key questions:

1. Can the majority of customer-facing personnel communicate the "elevator pitch" of your organization in a consistent and compelling fashion? If not, this is a clear indication that the right place to start—above all else—is a higher-level Why Change Whiteboard.

2. Are salespeople investing sales cycles in poorly qualified opportunities? Qualification and Discovery Whiteboards can help field personnel better prioritize which opportunities are worth investing sales cycles in.

3. Are sales opportunities being lost to "no decision" or "the status quo"? If so, a Why Change Whiteboard will help create a buying vision for your customer.

4. Are the near-term revenue goals and objectives of your organization disproportionately driven by a particular solution or product set? If so, a whiteboard directed at this solution will be well received by executives and sales leadership.

5. Are there particular solutions or products that salespeople gravitate toward based on how they are compensated? If a whiteboard story can help reps close more business for solutions that pay higher commissions or give them more quota credit, then the whiteboard's uptake will benefit.

6. Are there high revenue potential solutions and products that currently have low visibility among sales? If so, a whiteboard has the potential to raise awareness and open up or enhance new revenue streams for underserved products and solutions.

7. Is your sales organization pursuing new vertical markets or do you have a vertically aligned sales organization? Whiteboards designed to discuss solution value in the context of a particular vertical will address this alignment.

8. Have there been any recent acquisitions or mergers for which the rationale is unclear to either your sales force or customers? Whiteboards can be effectively used to educate salespeople and customers about how an acquisition, merger, or partnership makes business sense and benefits end customers.
9. Have a large number of new hires recently joined or will be joining the organization? We've worked with many organizations that rely on whiteboards as a mainstay of instructor-led new hire training.
10. Is there a particular competitor that is stealing market share or coming up over and over again in sales opportunities? In Chapter 13 we demonstrated a number of competitive whiteboards, which are often extremely popular with salespeople selling expensive solutions in highly competitive markets.

With all of the above options for whiteboard topics, how do you decide where to start? You could make a case that salespeople could derive significant benefit from any number of them. One of the easiest ways to decide is to survey your sales force using a web-based survey service. Your organization may already have a license to such a service.

The survey only needs to include a few questions. Here are some suggestions:

1. Would you like to see whiteboard stories developed that you can use in front of customers instead of slides? (Yes/No)
2. Which of the following topics would you like to see a whiteboard designed to cover? (Select three)
   (a) Solution A
   (b) Solution B
   (c) Solution C
   (d) Competitor A
   (e) Competitor B
   (f) Competitor C
   (g) Elevator Pitch
   (h) etc.

3. What other topics would you like to see covered by a whiteboard? (freeform text)
4. Do you have any whiteboard examples you currently use in sales situations? If so, can you please send a video, photo, or schematic to: (your e-mail)?

Question 1 can provide valuable data to garner executive support for whiteboard projects and initiatives. And question 4 will help identify any existing whiteboards that are being used "out in the wild," and that may provide valuable input into your efforts.

CHAPTER 19

Forming a Working Team

Few things in life are less efficient than a group of people trying to write a sentence. The advantage of this method is that you end up with something for which you will not be personally blamed.

—Scott Adams, creator of *Dilbert*

A working team for a whiteboard design initiative is different in purpose and makeup than a working team for other marketing and sales messaging projects.

Whiteboarding initiatives stir the passions of salespeople as a new and novel presentation mechanism, therefore they usually generate working teams whose members are from groups all over the company, not the least of which is sales. Sales is driving (and in some cases paying for) the whiteboard initiatives. This often results in sales executives who are willing to commit the time and resources of key members of their teams to participate and ensure that the whiteboard meets the needs of the field.

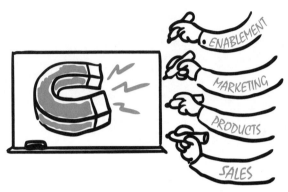

Even when whiteboarding projects are sponsored through marketing, sales is extremely interested and wants to participate. This is why whiteboarding projects are so effective in bridging the marketing and sales divide—whiteboarding finally brings together all the great work that marketing has done. It results in sales and marketing messaging delivered in a format and delivery model that appeals to salespeople. Salespeople want better ways to engage with their customers and prospects, and that is the result of a whiteboard initiative.

The net-net is that whiteboarding projects tend to have very high visibility across the organization, and there is usually very little difficulty in recruiting members.

The Working Team's Core Responsibilities

Here's what the working team does:

1. Defines whiteboard scope.
2. Gathers and confirms core messaging embodied by the whiteboard deliverable.

3. Drives and fully participates in the whiteboard design process.
4. Gathers input and approval from other key stakeholders and key players.
5. Provides leadership for, and participation in, whiteboard training events.

The time commitment for a working team member is approximately eight hours spread over a four- to five-week period, depending on the time frame of the project. This is very important to clarify when recruiting a working team member. You want to underscore the low-touch nature of the role. You don't want to distract your sales resources, whose chief responsibility is quota achievement and revenue generation.

Who Should Be on the Working Team?

So who exactly should be part of whiteboard project working teams?

We've seen a broad range of makeup and personalities in working teams. Much of it depends on the size of the organization. Smaller, earlier-stage clients have C-level executives and company founders as part of the working team. But even with customers that have sales forces in the many thousands, it is not uncommon to see VP-level marketing and sales executives as part of working teams.

Another driver of working team membership is a whiteboard's objectives and topics, discussed in Chapter 19. Once you have that nailed, selecting working team candidates is a fairly straightforward process. For higher-level, corporate stories, senior executives—who have a stake in the game when it comes to getting the story right—want to get involved. Senior titles are not usually involved with lower-level, more solution- or product-specific whiteboards or competitive whiteboards. There are sometimes exceptions, based on corporate culture. We worked with one very large Fortune 500 organization to design several whiteboards in parallel, and the working teams were packed with VP-level key players who had a fervent interest in the outcome of the project. What's more, the CEO of the company requested regular updates from the teams as the projects progressed.

So how big should a working team be? No fewer than five and no larger than eight members. With too few members there are not enough viewpoints and not enough representation of key constituencies. And when the working team gets into the double digits, you get the "too many cooks in the kitchen" syndrome going.

Working teams normally include individuals drawn from (but not limited to) the following profiles:

1. Marketing personnel (two people)
   (a) Solutions marketing managers
   (b) Product marketing managers
   (c) Directors of product marketing
   (d) Competitive intelligence analysts and managers
2. Field personnel (two or three people)
   (a) Top account managers (tenured, proven)
   (b) Top presales consultants and engineers
   (c) Sales manager or executive
3. Sales enablement and/or training (one person)
4. Product management (optional: one person)
   (a) Product manager
   (b) Director of product management
5. Evangelists and thought leaders

This last group includes "key players," who in many cases don't fit neatly into the other four groups. It is critical that these important influencers are sought out and at least invited to participate on the working team.

Product managers are marked as optional only because they (hopefully!) trust their marketing counterparts to represent their needs.

To summarize: If you are ever in doubt as to who should be on the working team for a whiteboard design project, just make sure that any message owners—key players who are instrumental in shaping the key corporate, solution, and even product messaging for your organization—are invited to participate.

Who *Shouldn't* Be on the Working Team?

The answer to this question is simple. If you invite someone, and they respond they are too busy to contribute the 8 to 10 hours over four to five weeks, then they shouldn't be on the team. The last thing you want is to have people sign up to participate and then not show up to key review meetings.

There is also a wider circle of people, such as field personnel and executives, whose input and approval you will need, but who are not essential working team members. In later sections we'll address ways you can get their input and sign off on the project.

ACTIVITY

With an initial whiteboard topic in mind, write down some working team candidate names using the above example titles.

So you have your Working Team formed, now what? You're about to embark on probably the most important part of the predesign process: selecting the ingredients that you are going to bake your whiteboard cake with.

CHAPTER 20

Taking a Message Inventory

You've chosen a whiteboard topic and formed your working team. You have your menu, your team of chefs, now all you need is the ingredients to prepare your masterpiece. You can't just run down to the corner grocer. You need prime ingredients from a gourmet food shop.

The majority of the organizations we work with have existing, effective messaging. Designing a whiteboard is not often an exercise of growing your own soybeans—it's more like the process to turn those soybeans into soy sauce, or make gasoline out of crude oil. [We shouldn't mix metaphors like this...stick to food metaphors...olive oil out of olives...wine out of grapes.]

However, there are cases where messaging is in flux rather than locked down. There are situations where an organization is going through a re-branding or re-messaging. Because the working team is x-functional in nature (including sales, marketing, training, etc.), the whiteboard design process is actually an opportunity to clarify and enhance certain aspects of that organization's messaging. There can be unanticipated benefits when the working team comes together. People begin to agree on common ground. What comes out of the process is consensus around important company themes, solution value messaging, and competitive positioning.

Content Requirements

Let's look at a situation where the raw materials are in place—the messaging is stable and mature—you just need to pick the ingredients off the shelf after you find out which aisle they're on. The type of content required will correspond with the scope of the whiteboard and the corresponding messaging. If it is a higher-level Why Change Whiteboard, you'll need a very broad set of materials that cover all of your organization's solutions and services. A more specific Solution Whiteboard that focuses on a specific solution or category of offerings (by industry, use case, etc.) will require a much narrower set of content.

★ LEVEL 1
INGREDIENTS

LEVEL 2
INGREDIENTS

Let's take a closer look at six sources of messaging you'll want to assemble with the help of the working team.

1. *Core solution sales and marketing presentations (PPT or PDF).* These are the official sales presentations, executive briefing decks, and other fully-sanctioned customer-facing materials that have been blessed by the powers that be. It is extremely important that the final whiteboard story—while not having to perfectly align with these materials—should reflect and embrace their core themes and message pillars. One of the arts of whiteboard design is how to take one of these 25, 30, or even 50-plus slide presentations, and reduce it to its essence on a "single pane" image that a salesperson can deliver in 10 minutes or less.

2. *Product/solution messaging contained in Word documents or Excel spreadsheets.* This can include any "message maps" that were put together before the sales and marketing presentations.

3. *"Sales play" or playbook documents.* Whether tied to a specific sales methodology or homegrown, sales playbooks or "sales motion" tools may be valuable sources of messaging and other content for the whiteboard, including key questions to ask the customer during an interactive dialogue.

4. *"Battle cards"* and *"cheat sheets."* These sales tools are perfect ingredients for whiteboarding because they provide sales with bite-sized talking points, silver bullets, and probing questions. Some organizations build these tools in a parallel effort to the whiteboard design because the same design principles are in play—easily digested and easily communicated "knowledge nuggets" that resonate with customers and spark a two-way information exchange.

5. *Competitive documents (presentations, Word docs, PDFs).* Anything with the word "competitive" in it will prove extremely useful in the design process as most if not all whiteboards should have at least *some* competitive element to them.

6. *Existing whiteboard concepts.* Some of the most important whiteboard ingredients are home-cooked visual stories used by salespeople and other customer-facing personnel. Put your feelers out early to identify these storyboards. They are often used with great success but without much fanfare or exposure to others in the organization. If you make an effort to bring these whiteboarding examples and those who designed them into the process, you will create important project ambassadors and champions.

This is only a narrow subset of the possible content sources for the key whiteboard ingredients. Depending on the topic and scope of the whiteboard, you will need to rely on your working team to guide you and provide you with additional information sources.

CHAPTER 21

The Working Team Template

Once you've formed your working team and assembled the core messaging assets, it's time for the working team to roll up its collective sleeves and distill the raw materials into the essential whiteboard ingredients. In previous sections we've shared examples of finished products and identified some of the key ingredients at a high level. But in this chapter we will go into detail on each ingredient and explain the specific role it plays.

That process starts with what we call a *working team template*, a structured document to ensure everything that needs to be considered as part of the whiteboard design project is taken into account. The template doesn't just capture the ingredients that go into the whiteboard. It also captures who you are serving the food to, who the waitstaff are, and which food critics have written you up.

The template also includes elements we have already covered in previous sections, such as whiteboarding objectives, leveling, and scope.

But in this chapter we will focus on those components we haven't explored yet. Keep in mind that these whiteboard ingredients aren't all used at the same time in the various whiteboard types we've discussed. You can refer back to each example to see where they are—and are not—included.

Here are the elements of the working team template:

1. Whiteboard development objectives
2. Whiteboard leveling and scope
3. Whiteboard name
4. Target complete date
5. Whiteboard audience
6. Delivered by roles
7. High-level market trends and themes
8. Company/solution unique capabilities
9. Competitive focus and silver bullet
10. Key references and case studies
11. Third-party recognition

We've already covered numbers one and two, so we'll start with whiteboard name.

Whiteboard Name

Each whiteboard should have a name that can be used to identify it within the organization. Having a catchy or memorable name can help increase the visibility of the whiteboard and the overall initiative.

For example, one company we worked with had a whiteboard story that became affectionately known as "The Diamond Pitch," due to the fact that the basic structure of the whiteboard was in the shape of a diamond, with the solution in the middle and the various product components arrayed around it in four facets. Once developed and partly distributed to the sales force, the Diamond Pitch took on a life of its own within the organization, due in part to the intrigue associated with its name. It also developed more cachet value with executives, who began stating, "I want everyone certified on the Diamond Pitch," inferring that the whiteboard was the gold standard way to represent the company's solutions and services.

The lesson here is that adding a memorable name can help you create a brand around the whiteboarding. And putting an interesting visual twist on a whiteboard can provide the fodder for an interesting name.

More generic whiteboard name examples include:

- The [COMPANY] Story Whiteboard
- The [COMPANY] Vision Whiteboard
- Selling Value with [SOLUTION]
- The [COMPANY/SOLUTION/PRODUCT] Whiteboard

Target Complete Date

An average whiteboard design process takes a minimum of approximately five weeks. An effective practice is to work backwards from a compelling event, such as a training session where the whiteboard is going to be introduced to sales. Make sure to leave approximately one week to print whiteboard training tools. If the source messaging content is extremely comprehensive and baked, and if the time frame, resources, and other workload commitments are available, a whiteboard can be completed in as few as three weeks.

Whiteboard Audience

Who is the audience for the whiteboard? In earlier sections we provided a number of examples of different types of whiteboards, but none of them are designed for a specific audience type (with the exception of the Closing Whiteboard, which is targeted at a high-level, economic buyer). All Solution Whiteboards, for example, should be designed to be multilevel, i.e., consumable by C-level audiences down to managers. Even though the whiteboard is consumed by different audiences, the story structure and flow of the whiteboard need to remain consistent. What may change is the amount, and in some cases the nature, of the content that is left up on the board after the meeting.

As it relates to audience, two factors determine what the final board looks like:

1. *The amount of time a salesperson has in front of a prospect.* The more time, the more detail and amount of content presented; the general story structure should not change.
2. *The level of your audience.* If you are presenting to a busy C-level executive, you should use a shorter and content-light whiteboard, regardless of whiteboard type.

For example, take Emeril Lagasse's recipe for Chicken Marsala:

$1/2$ cup all-purpose flour
1 tablespoon Essence
2 (6- to 8-ounce) boneless, skinless chicken breasts, cut in halves and pounded thin
1 tablespoon olive oil
4 tablespoons butter
3 cups sliced mushrooms (cremini, oyster, shiitake)
$3/4$ cup Marsala wine

1 cup chicken stock
Salt and freshly ground black pepper
Chopped chives, for garnish

There are a lot of ingredients and steps in this recipe. Now let's take a look at a much simpler recipe for the same dish:

1 tablespoon butter
6 skinless, boneless chicken breasts
1 (10.75 ounce) can condensed golden mushroom soup
1-$\frac{1}{4}$ cups Marsala wine

There are some common ingredients (butter, chicken, and Marsala wine), but the second example lacks the fresh mushrooms, chicken stock, chives, and of course, Emeril's Essence! But the benefit is that you can prepare the second example in about a third of the time as Emeril's. The same goes for a whiteboard. The structure and flow of the whiteboard (the overall physical presentation of the dish) is roughly approximate, but the amount of content and detail (ingredients, taste, and texture) will vary.

Delivered by Roles

Who within your organization (specific titles) will be delivering the whiteboard story to end customers? This is typically determined by the whiteboard leveling. Why Change Whiteboards and higher-level Solution Whiteboards are often more easily presented by a much broader group within the organization, including field-facing personnel, channel partners, and even high-level executives. As we will discuss in Chapter 27, even inside sales personnel can now present various types of whiteboards with customers using remote whiteboarding technology.

High-Level Market Trends and Themes

In order to present a whiteboard, you must own the knowledge. This means that whiteboarding positions you as a thought leader and trusted advisor. But you can't just start off a meeting by whiteboarding out your solution. You need to create common ground with your customer by demonstrating you are well educated about the major market trends, themes, and challenges that are relevant to the discussion.

- What is the industry saying?
- What are the third-party analysts, trade publications, or ranking firms talking about?
- How do your competitors frame the market drivers?
- What are your other customers thinking about?

Your prospect is likely relying on these same sources as well, attending trade shows, reading relevant websites, and talking with peers. You must be aware of and have command of these trends and themes if you are going to earn the right to continue the information exchange and progress through the sales cycle with senior-level buyers. These trends and themes will also help determine which corporate and solution-level messaging to highlight in the whiteboard. And remember, if sellers can teach buyers something they didn't already know about, the trust factor will skyrocket.

Company/Solution Capabilities

This section of the Messaging Template is probably the most important. What are the core company and solution capabilities that need to be highlighted in the whiteboard? These need to provide unique and measurable values that other competing solutions cannot deliver. Try to stay away from in-depth discussion of features and functions.

If you refer to the case study we used to demonstrate the whiteboard template examples, Cool Road Trucking had a number of unique capabilities that competing solutions lacked.

Full Life Cycle Services

Cool Road is the only national provider that offers a combination of refrigerated equipment, tracking and monitoring, equipment maintenance, emergency services, and end-product sourcing.

One Point of Contact

Cool Road is the only company to provide a single point of contact for all issues related to sourcing, delivery, and monitoring.

Nationwide Network

Cool Road offers one of the largest networks of temperature-controlled hubs and collection points, with 118 hubs in 36 states.

TempTrust

Competing refrigeration control systems are bolted onto existing semis, but Cool Road's temperature control units are built into—and fully integrated with—trucking equipment.

CleanCool

Cool Road is the only refrigerated trucking company that has the capability to limit emissions of dangerous chemicals and other toxic compounds.

Company/Solution Capabilities Must be "Binary"

These capabilities and defining characteristics are binary. Either you have them or you don't. Either your temperature control systems are integrated or they are not. Either you have a nationwide network or you don't. Either you provide a full life cycle of capabilities or you only focus on trucking.

You want to avoid capabilities and features that are not differentiating and may even get sales resources into trouble during a whiteboard discussion. Here are some examples:

1. Cool Road's trucks ride smoother than the competition's, which leads to less damage to cargo. Prospect's response: "Really? How do you measure that? Do you have breakage statistics compared to competing solutions?" In other words, this is a subjective element, not a binary one, and could lead to an awkward moment at best and a delayed sales cycle at worst. On the other hand, CleanCool is a unique technology and can measure emissions reductions compared to national averages.
2. Cool Road's drivers are better trained than the competition's. Prospect's response: "Really? How are they trained and how is that better? How do your competitors train their drivers?"
3. Cool Road has the newest fleet in the industry. Customer's response: "Really? Do you have data to support that?"

You get the idea. You want to select capabilities to include in your whiteboard that clearly separate you from the competition in a binary, yes/no fashion. For example, if you know that the competitor has a nationwide network, you won't feature that in your whiteboard because it is not differentiating. When we work with our customers, we often have to put a lot of effort into identifying these truly unique elements. The binary rule doesn't just apply to whiteboarding, but to any type of marketing or sales tools. But with a whiteboard, you don't have the luxury of cycling through 30 slides that describe all of your features and functions. You need to be highly selective about what you talk about within the space provided.

ACTIVITY

On a blank piece of paper, create two columns. In the right-hand column, make a list of the binary differentiating elements/capabilities of your company, solution, or product. In the left hand column, list some of the subjective or nonsupportable items.

Competitive Focus and Silver Bullets

Even basic Solution Whiteboards should have a competitive element to them. If you are designing a Competitive Whiteboard that focuses on a specific competitor, you should identify the key points of differentiation and silver bullets specific to that competitor. In the example of the *Typical Approaches* Competitive Whiteboard, there are competitive deficiencies common across a number of competitors, when compared to the unique value and capabilities of your solutions and services. You can usually find this data within most marketing and sales organizations, but you need to verify each silver bullet with trusted field resources to ensure they still apply and are binary and defensible.

There are exceptions to the binary rule within the context of a competitive whiteboard. If you are late to market or up against an established competitor that may be further down the sales cycle with your prospect, you may need to use a competitive whiteboard to "level the playing field." You can highlight capabilities you know the customer needs and that the competing vendor also offers. You've earned the right to stay in the race. Then you can go for the jugular with your unique, binary capabilities.

Key References and Case Studies

All whiteboards—regardless of level or topic—must include proof. You need to show where your company and your solutions have been successfully engaged or implemented, preferably by brand-name organizations. Key references and case studies are often one of the most important content requirements. You can often get these directly from marketing teams or salespeople. Make sure you have permission to use the customer's name. If you don't have permission, you can refer to the reference obliquely, such as "large food store chain based in Chicago."

If at all possible, use proven success information that is measurable, such as "increased revenue by 25 percent," or "a 50 percent reduction in operating expenses," or "reduced implementation time by two hours." In our case study, Cool Road Trucking's customer FoodAllRight's "time-2-store" delivery metric was reduced by 22 percent. Providing measurable benefits is far superior to saying, "FoodAllRight experienced decreased delivery times."

Leading with case studies and references is also a great way to open up a whiteboard dialogue, because it piques the interest of your prospects even before the knowledge exchange moves to a deeper level.

Third-Party Recognition

Just as important as proven success is third-party recognition of your organization. This could include industry analyst firms, luminaries, or other third parties who have reviewed, endorsed, awarded, or otherwise validated your company and solutions. These endorsements complement references and case studies and are important validation points used in the whiteboard stories. If you recall, Cool Road Trucking was recently awarded *FridgeRoad Magazine's* #1 rating and a *RideCold Rating* Top Pick.

So now you've got your ingredients and are ready to bake your cake. But you'll need just a few instructions on how to mix them all together. We'll look at that in the next chapter, "Formalizing Your Whiteboard Design."

CHAPTER 22

Formalizing Your Whiteboard Design

The dumbest mistake is viewing design as something you do at the end of the process to "tidy up" the mess, as opposed to understanding it's a "day one" issue and part of everything.

—Tom Peters

Tom Peters' insight is instructive as it informs the design focus of many of the whiteboard structures we have featured in this book. The "day one issue," as Peters put it, is the design element that corresponds to current market trends and themes, as well as to the customer's challenges and business issues, and *not* your solution or services. This design point is what enables the discussion to be situationally driven by the customer.

You've put in place the resources (content and people) required to be successful with a whiteboard project. Now you are in a position to formalize your whiteboard design. If you've completed the exercises and activities in earlier chapters, it will be a fairly easy exercise to combine that work with some basic design best practices.

Basic Whiteboard Design Guidelines

First, there are a number of important guidelines and principles that we suggest be adhered to when designing a whiteboard story for sales. Here are eight of these guidelines as they apply to a Solution Whiteboard:

1. Whiteboards are single-pane visual narratives. What this means is that, unlike a traditional storyboard, a whiteboard for sales—at least from our perspective—does not occupy separate "canvases." It should be a cohesive visual that tells a singular story within a defined space—either on an actual whiteboard, on a flipchart, on a small section of butcher paper at a restaurant over lunch with your customer, or on any other drawing surface.

2. Likewise, whiteboards do not have components that are erased when the whiteboard is delivered, for similar reasons to number one above. After the whiteboard is delivered to your customer or prospect (who, you hope, writes "save" or "do not erase" next to it) and you leave, anyone else who walks into that office or conference room should be able to take a look at the visual and get a pretty clear sense of the story you are trying to tell. Erasing elements as you go along would be akin to literally tearing chapters out of a book.

3. Typically, a whiteboard is broken up into between 6 and 12 steps, each step equating to a chapter in a book. Each step should address a specific part of the storyline. For example, "Market Trends and Themes" would typically have its own step, as would "Next Steps and Actions."

4. An effective Solution Whiteboard should contain no more than 75 words on the visual.

5. Whiteboards should contain more than just words, so we suggest a bit of "eye candy" in the way of simple drawings or iconography. The whiteboard templates in Section 3 provide good examples, and a well-designed whiteboard should contain as few as 5 but no more than 10 to 12 visual elements (not including lines, circles, and other basic shapes).
6. Each whiteboard step should have no more than 400 words of scripting, and should take between 1 and 1.5 minutes to present, uninterrupted.
7. Each whiteboard step should have at least one question to ask and one Objection Reframe. (See Chapter 23 for more details.)
8. Effective whiteboards can be drawn in just one color (black or blue are usually recommended), but the use of multiple colors can be effective. For example, the whiteboard examples in this book more often than not use black to frame the discussion and describe solutions, and red to depict customer challenges and competitive weaknesses. A four-color scheme can also be effective:
   (a) Black to frame the discussion.
   (b) Red for business challenges or competitive limitations.
   (c) Green for your solutions.
   (d) Blue for references, anecdotes, and third-party validation.

The advantage of four colors is that someone observing the whiteboard for the first time *after* it has been drawn can get a pretty good sense of the narrative just based on the colors used.

One additional note on colors: As your whiteboard flows from step to step, make sure that your design does not require frequent color changes within each step. This would make it more difficult for sellers to present the whiteboard and would definitely complicate the whiteboard training process.

ACTIVITY

Select two or three of the whiteboards you designed in the last section and, using a blank sheet of paper, redraw the whiteboard, keeping in mind the design guidelines outlined above, and use the appropriate colors. Remember those Bic four-color ballpoint pens you used back in high school? Well, guess what, Bic still makes them, so go down to your nearby office supply store and pick up a few, since they work great for whiteboard prototyping.

CHAPTER 23

Packaging Your Whiteboard

Once you have a whiteboard design you are happy with, or a set of whiteboards aligned with each of the whiteboard types we have discussed, it's time to "productionize" your whiteboard so it is consumable by your field personnel and others intended to deliver the whiteboard in the course of business. You've written a script aligned with each step of the whiteboard as described in Chapter 22, but there are still five steps to make your whiteboard sales-ready.

1. Creating professional visuals.
2. Adding key questions to ask.
3. Adding Objection Reframes.
4. Packaging your whiteboard into sales tools.
5. Recording whiteboard videos and animations.

   Let's talk about each of these.

Creating Professional Visuals

While we have the benefit of icon libraries, design templates, and professional whiteboard design software to manage content and generate whiteboard sales tools, a do-it-yourself approach to giving your whiteboard high production values is not insurmountable. Ironically, PowerPoint is an ideal platform to lay out your whiteboard text and iconography. Anyone with a pen-enabled Windows-based laptop/tablet running PowerPoint 2010 or later can take advantage of PowerPoint's pen annotation feature. Even those without a pen-enabled system can use the "Pens" Quick Access Toolbar command to draw pen annotations using the mouse. Here are the six steps required to do this:

1. Right-click on the Quick Access Toolbar (located either above or below the Ribbon) and select "Customize Quick Access Toolbar."
2. Select "All Commands" under "Choose Commands" in the "Power-Point Options" dialog box.
3. Scroll down to the "Pens" command.
4. Click on the "Add" button to move the Pens command into your list of commands.
5. Once it shows up in your Quick Access Toolbar, clicking on the Pens command allows you to select a pen color and width.
6. Using your mouse, draw your shape and notice the "anti-aliasing" feature that will smooth out jagged lines.

You aren't limited to using PowerPoint, and graphic designers familiar with professional design software can use pen tablets to draw iconography and other visuals. The key is to maintain a whiteboard drawing style for the visuals and create them in a fashion that is easy enough for a salesperson to draw without much practice.

Adding Key Questions to Ask

As mentioned in earlier chapters, it is critical to build interactivity into whiteboards for sales, which are designed to promote a two-way information exchange. The most effective way to do this is to write several questions that salespeople can ask during each step of the whiteboard conversation. Let's look at how questions can be integrated into the *Today versus Tomorrow* Why Change Whiteboard example we demonstrated in Chapter 12.

When presenting the Why Change section of the whiteboard, questions a salesperson might ask a customer could include:

"In what parts of your product mix are you seeing the most spoilage and revenue loss due to shipping delays?"
"How are temperature variations during shipping impacting spoilage rates?"

You will notice we try to avoid yes/no questions since they can lead to an opportunity for a prospect to simply roadblock the discussion. Open-ended questions can also be thought-provoking and get the customer to think about things they haven't yet assessed.

During the Why Now section, a key question could be:

"What alternatives have you considered to FTL (Full Truck Load) shipping for fresh foods from farm to store?"

This kind of question can get your prospect thinking about alternatives that play into your strengths. In this case, one of Cool Road's core competencies is Less Than Truck Load shipping, which decreases spoilage and decreases time-to-store.

When it comes to discussing the customer proof point, an obvious question would be, "We have customers who have seen decreased shipping times and reduced spoilage compared to traditional shipping solutions. Would speaking with them be useful in your evaluation process?" In this case, a yes/no question is appropriate because it is a direct question about a proposed action item.

Adding Objection Reframes

During any sales presentation or discussion—whether using Power-Point, a whiteboard, or just sitting with your prospect over lunch—you'll always get objections. Seasoned salespeople usually know how to handle even the most difficult objections. But new hires and less experienced sellers can benefit from coaching, and accompanying the whiteboarding sales tools with objection handlers is a great opportunity to enhance the whiteboard dialogue. Effectively handling objections can only help build trusted advisor status.

Looking at the Why Now section of the *Today versus Tomorrow* Why Change Whiteboard, a typical objection might be,

Our shipping operations may not be the most efficient, but they've been in place for years now and there would be a lot of risk and potential disruption caused by a switch to a Less-Than-Truckload approach.

An appropriate reframe might be,

That's a valid concern, and Food-All-Right had the same fear before we moved them to a more efficient model. We have proven transition planning models that can gradually move you off an FTL model without any disruption. All you will see is gradually declining spoilage rates.

ACTIVITY

Using the *Today versus Tomorrow* Whiteboard example you put together earlier, create two questions and two objection reframes for each of the four motions of the whiteboard.

Packaging Your Whiteboard into Sales Tools

You should now have professional whiteboard visuals for each step or chapter in your whiteboard, as well as scripting, questions to ask, and objection reframes. You now need to come up with sales tools that encompass these whiteboard elements and make the whiteboard consumable and learnable by sales. You can use any of the Microsoft Office or Adobe products, or work with your creative team to come up with layouts and whiteboard guides to bring everything together. These tools should be easy to navigate and be usable in the hands of sellers as they practice at the whiteboard, and if possible should conform to the branding and color/font guidelines of other sales tools and materials distributed to sales. If possible, whiteboard tools should be printed on heavy stock or laminated, not just color copies on standard weight paper.

It is also important to note that whiteboard tools are typically used solely by sales to learn the whiteboard content before, during, and after whiteboard training, and are not intended for external consumption by customers and prospects.

Recording Whiteboard Videos

In additional to physical whiteboarding tools for sales, you may consider recording videos of the whiteboard being presented by a subject matter expert. You can also record a video of yourself drawing the whiteboard onscreen using digital paper (discussed in Chapter 27) and using a variety of screen capture programs.

These videos can be excellent training tools for existing sellers, and are especially valuable for new hires. They can be used as part of e-learning modules and may even be leveraged as external, customer-facing marketing assets for lead generation and other programs.

If you are going to video yourself or someone else presenting the whiteboard, the following are some practical guidelines to ensure the video is professional and ready for distribution. Even if you have a professional crew or video studio, these 17 guidelines will be useful.

1. Any low-cost HD video camera will do, even the Flip Video type devices mounted on small tripods. Just make sure you have plenty of storage space, either internal to the device or using an external SD card or Micro SD card storage.

2. Identify a quiet, well-lit conference room with a full-size whiteboard (wall-mounted or freestanding) within five feet or less of the conference table.

3. Do not wear stripes or pure black—solid earth tones and blue colors are preferred.

4. Using the tripod, use a straight-on shot/camera angle; experiment with angles to minimize shadows.

5. Stand perpendicular to the whiteboard.

6. Using your black dry erase marker, mark off four corners of the drawing space with four faint dots to ensure the whiteboard drawing remains within the camera frame.

7. If possible, avoid including whiteboard borders or metal frames in the camera shot.

8. Put a chair behind you to keep yourself from moving out of the video frame.

9. Put tape, a water bottle, or other object in front of your foot as a reminder to stay within the camera frame.

10. Use 720p video quality setting.

11. Experiment with audio settings to yield the best quality (you can optionally wear a clip-on microphone, either physically connected to the camera or wireless).

12. Film each clip associated with each whiteboard step, stopping the camera between each step; retake steps as necessary; mark each clip with "clip x, take x."

13. Feel free to refer to your whiteboard sales tool in between takes to ensure you are following the structure, flow, and content (iconography, etc.) of the whiteboard story. However, memorization of the whiteboard script is not required, and in fact is discouraged. You want to demonstrate how important it is that presenters use their own language and presentation style when delivering the whiteboard talk track.

14. *Important*—take care to erase only what is drawn during a step prior to a retake of that step. Erasing previous step contents will require a complete reshoot.

15. Talk while you write (then turn to the camera and expand on the topic).

16. Put caps on whiteboard markers in between use to avoid drying them out.

17. Good penmanship helps, and slowing down 5 to 10 percent will work wonders.

ACTIVITY

With the help of a colleague, find a conference room and video yourself presenting the whiteboard.

PART 5

Enabling the Field

CHAPTER 24

Whiteboard Test Drive

et's recap where we are so far, in the following six steps:

1. You are by now convinced that visual storytelling is a better way to foster a two-way dialogue, build trust, and communicate unique value to your customers and prospects compared to slides (if not, go back and reread Parts 1 and 2, or put down the book).
2. You are familiar with the various whiteboard types (No? Please turn back to Part 3.)
3. You've put in place the resources (content and people) required to be successful with a whiteboard project.
4. You have confirmed your existing messaging and broken it out into the necessary whiteboarding ingredients using the Working Team Template.
5. You've spent about a month iterating with your working team to ensure your story is on point and achieves the whiteboard objectives you established at the beginning of the process, and you've gotten

buyoff from higher level executives and stakeholders that the whiteboard narrative is consistent with their view of the organization's overarching strategic objectives and initiatives.

6. You have designed and packaged one or more of the whiteboard examples showcased in earlier chapters, and perhaps even videotaped yourself or a colleague delivering the whiteboard.

So now what? It would seem intuitive to roll out your whiteboard tools and videos, and begin formal enablement programs to train sellers on how to deliver the whiteboard in a confident, compelling, and consistent fashion to prospects and customers. Well, not so fast.

In just six weeks from the time the design was started, we had the motor on the block testing its power.

—Orville Wright

What is ironic—or more important, instructive—about Orville Wright's quotation is that it takes about four to six weeks to design and iterate on an individual whiteboard, complete with visuals, script, questions to ask, and objections and how to reframe them. But testing its power is a crucial step prior to fully packaging it and launching it using wide scale enablement programs.

Regardless of your role in your organization, there are four key constituencies you need to test your whiteboard in front of, in the following order:

1. Trusted partners
2. Existing customers
3. Other third parties or industry analysts
4. Sales

The order in which you conduct this focus testing is critical.

1. *Trusted Partners* may include resellers, affiliates, or other closely associated individuals and entities that represent your organization, solutions, and services. These people sometimes know your solutions better than your own sellers, and they may have a unique perspective on customer buying criteria, market trends, and your unique differentiators. In fact, some customers we have worked with include business partners on working teams, although this is the exception rather than the rule. At the very least, partners may be asked to provide input during the design process in the form of one-hour remote web conferences or other informal meetings, to ensure you are on the right path with your whiteboard design, key themes, and content. Partners will be brutally honest about your whiteboard deliverable, and will help you calibrate design elements and scripting. Getting partner feedback can be done in person or remotely.

2. *Existing Customers.* Once you have incorporated changes suggested by business partners, it is time to informally showcase your whiteboard with a trusted, existing customer who you know can provide honest feedback. This is best done in person, not only so you can gauge reactions, but it is also an opportunity to get some face time with your customer and perhaps do some cross-sell or up-sell. In our experience, existing customers are most useful in providing input around your whiteboard's key market trends, typical challenges, and unique differentiators. They can also provide guidance on typical objections and key questions to ask. Rarely do we find that customers will completely reject a whiteboard design structure and story flow. More often, in addition to validating and suggesting changes to your existing whiteboard, they will suggest other whiteboard topics and types that you can put in your future whiteboard design plans.

3. *Third Parties and Industry Analysts.* Depending on the type of solutions and services you sell and your industry, your organization may

subscribe to the services of an analyst firm or other third-party ratings organization, and you may have regular access to their experts. In this case, you may elect to run your whiteboard by them, as you would any other sales and marketing messaging you are in the process of developing. In many cases, analysts are regularly briefed during the message creation process, which typically occurs before a whiteboard is designed, in which case they will most likely not have any major objections from a content perspective. Keep in mind, however, that many industry analysts have distinct points of view and strong opinions, and they could suggest taking a completely different approach to your whiteboard. Take this feedback with a grain of salt, since your whiteboard has already gone through a lot of focus testing. What you are looking for is similar to the feedback you might get from a customer. Most important, you are looking for any type of violent reaction to your whiteboard messaging, themes, story flow, and other components.

4. *Sales.* Now that you have input/validation from partners, trusted customers, and in some cases third-party analysts and other firms (and have incorporated their suggested changes or additions), you are in a very strong position to organize a limited pilot whiteboard training of between 8 and 12 sellers. Your pilot program will exactly mirror the enablement session you plan to roll out more broadly, as will be discussed at a high level in the next chapter.

ACTIVITY

Using one of the whiteboard examples you put together earlier, road test your whiteboard on at least one trusted business partner and an existing customer. Document their feedback, but before incorporating it into your whiteboard design and content, share your findings with your working team to get their input and blessing.

CHAPTER 25

Field Enablement Options

The Whiteboard Selling approach provides a sales training and enable-ment model unlike any I've witnessed. Most sales training approaches are heavy on process and light on how to actually communicate solu-tion value to customers and prospects at the point of sale. Whiteboard Selling, on the other hand, is entirely focused on how to engage in con-fident and compelling C-level communications with interactive, visual presentations. This visual storytelling approach to sales enablement is ideal to ensure that enterprise sales personnel are elite executive presenters—ready and able to make corporate messaging relevant and well-differentiated from the competition.

—Christopher Thomas, VP Sales, CA Technologies

Once a whiteboard pilot is completed and feedback incorporated, you are now in a position to confidently launch whiteboard train-ing to the field. Developing a whiteboard is a great first step, but stopping there really misses the whole point of the endeavor, which is equipping sales with a set of tools, skills, and ultimately that critical element of knowledge ownership to raise their game when engaging with customers and prospects with confidence. The question is, when can you start seeing ROI from the whiteboard design phase? The answer is whiteboarding enablement.

Whiteboard enablement and training for the field comes in many flavors, but the ultimate goal is twofold. The first is to enable sales to have mastery of the whiteboard content, structure, flow, key questions to ask, and objections and how to reframe them. The second objective is to provide basic whiteboarding skills and best practices, as discussed in Part 6. Content mastery together with whiteboarding skills results in a seller's ability to confidently present a visual story to a customer or prospect and have an interactive information exchange.

There are six enablement options that can be put in place to get sales teams ramped up on how to use the whiteboards:

1. Large-scale whiteboard symposiums
2. Regional whiteboard symposiums
3. Remote whiteboard symposiums
4. Online learning paths
5. E-learning
6. New hire training

The Whiteboard Symposium Approach

In earlier sections we referenced studies that consistently show training participants retain about 70 to 90 percent of material when learning in a hands-on, visual fashion—in other words, with pen in hand. The Whiteboard Symposium enablement option is not just about whiteboard memorization—it is designed to be a role-play-based learning mechanism to transfer solution knowledge quickly and effectively to field personnel who may not possess the situational fluency and deep domain expertise of tenured and proven sales resources. As of this writing, we have put over 50,000 globally-distributed sellers through the symposium approach, in groups as few as a dozen to as many as several thousand at a time. These events—which can be half-day, full-day, or even multiday activities—are ideal for sales kickoffs and other large-scale sales gatherings that are typically loaded with slide presentation trainings about the latest and greatest product features and functions.

The symposium events are based on what we call the Unit of Six: six participants per table, working together as a team and leveraging a role-play-based, repetitive, simulated sales call approach to present the whiteboard to one another using a flipchart and markers. The role-play sessions are preceded by a "why-whiteboard" keynote and a gold-standard presentation of the whiteboard presentation delivered by a sales leader or other subject matter expert. The beauty of the Unit of Six is that it can scale from two tables up to several hundred tables or more (space permitting!). The events are capped off by a competition of top performers in front of the entire group.

Large-Scale Whiteboard Symposium Case Study

One of our largest customers—a leading virtualization software vendor —enabled over 3,000 front-line field personnel in a single sales kickoff event, taking over the entire conference center of a large Las Vegas hotel and casino. Our customer saw explosive growth over the past few years, including major additions to their global field organization. In the midst of this hiring—and as part of their own broad-reaching sales transformation initiative—they needed a way to enable and train their global field organization on the new company positioning, messaging, and value proposition, so they could more effectively sell solutions to C-level buyers, and differentiate from the competition by not relying on slides.

Their requirement for the kickoff was to leverage a more creative approach to engage field personnel in hands-on exercises instead of more slide presentations on the latest and greatest features and functions. The event was a major success, with the majority of the participants leaving with the ability to present the whiteboard the very next day.

When surveyed, participants identified three factors that contributed to their overwhelming satisfaction with the enablement sessions:

1. The sessions were interactive, with participants able to ask questions, add things to the whiteboard, and share their opinions while learning from others.
2. The training was 100 percent hands-on, facilitating active learning.
3. The activities encouraged team members to come out of their comfort zone to learn new skills and present in ways they did not think possible.

The whiteboard enablement was such a success at the kickoff that our customer immediately began enabling its partners with the material, and localizing the content into seven different languages.

The Regional Symposium Approach

Unfortunately, although whiteboard symposiums make a big splash at large-scale sales kickoffs that need that something special to motivate the troops and foster team building, these types of meetings usually only happen once a year. What's more, many companies are moving away from these events due to cost cutting measures. Another of our customers—an even larger organization—chose a similar symposium model, the difference being that the training teams traveled to each sales region and ran half-day events for groups of 100 to 150. The regional GMs used the balance of the day for account reviews, sales planning, and other activities. These events are just as successful, and also benefit from a more intimate setting and team-specific focus.

Remote Symposiums

Imagine 50 different locations spread across the globe, with groups of as few as four and as many as several dozen, participating in a remote symposium experience that follows the same team-based model as an in-person event. We conducted one such event for more than 700 participants in a single five-hour session. A "home-base" location is run by the symposium facilitator, remotely guiding the group through the activity and exercises. Inexpensive, high-definition webcams are used in each location, joined together in a web meeting environment that enables the host to switch focus between locations to collaborate, share whiteboard examples, and even run competitions. In certain respects, remote symposiums have advantages over large scale and regional events: they significantly reduce costs, and actually allow for a more personalized experience because of the moderator's ability to zoom in on a specific location's team and share whiteboard examples. An additional consideration for a remote symposium is the requirement for a local facilitator at each location.

Online Learning Paths

Organized symposiums—whether in person or remote—are excellent opportunities for teams to come together, share knowledge, and learn from each other. You also have the built-in advantage of monitoring the learning experience to ensure uptake of the whiteboard content. But in some cases, team-based training is just not an option. Or, some organizations want to complement in-person events with online learning as prework, or as an event follow-up requirement. This is where the concept of an Online Learning Path can be very effective. Online Learning Paths are not a new concept, as they leverage industry-standard LMSs (Learning Management Systems) to serve up content to individual sellers or other field resources. For learning a whiteboard, they can be very effective, and they follow a prescribed ordering of these six activities:

1. Register for the online module.
2. Complete prereading on the topic of the whiteboard (using live links to content).
3. Take a quiz on the prereading.
4. Once the quiz is passed, watch a video of the whiteboard, either being delivered by an individual or through simulated whiteboard drawing.
5. Take another quiz on the content of the whiteboard.
6. Receive a certificate of completion.

Online Learning Paths usually track registration and provide reporting on completion status, requiring some level of setup and monitoring. But with this comes the benefit of ensuring total participation in either a stand-alone training delivery model or as pre/post work in conjunction with a symposium event.

Online Learning Paths for whiteboard training and enablement are also a great option for partner enablement and certification. Several of our customers used the Online Learning Path approach to ensure partners achieved the necessary level of solution knowledge, and whiteboard mastery was one of the required tracks to achieve Platinum status (which came with certain benefits, such as increased margin, etc.).

E-Learning Modules

A simplified version of an Online Learning Path is simply an E-Learning module that might include a video of the whiteboard and some accompanying slides. These types of modules may or may not require registration and tracking.

New Hire Training

Many of our customers build whiteboard symposiums and even online training into their standard new-hire curriculums. One such customer does not allow a new hire seller to "touch" a customer until they are certified on three different Solution Whiteboards.

CHAPTER 26

Measuring Success

All the clients were very impressed. In some of the opportunities they took pictures or asked me not to clean the white board. It was impressive. They loved it, and plan to use it themselves as the basis for telling their own story "up the ladder" to the committee that approves their funding. The whiteboard got the customer to start identifying areas of opportunity. It expanded their understanding of what was possible.

—Enterprise Seller Symposium Participant

One of the most often-asked questions we get when proposing Whiteboard Selling to prospects as a way to increase knowledge ownership, improve confidence, sell higher, and close more/bigger deals, is, "So, show me the ROI." We submit that it is no easy task for any sales methodology or other training approach to take credit for *quantitative* sales metric improvements. While it is possible in rare cases to confidently correlate a single set of skills or a new way of selling with sales improvements, we believe making blanket statements is in most cases deceptive selling. We frequently observe methodology and training vendors claiming that they "increased sales by x" or "improved deal close rates by y."

There are so many other factors that can contribute to fluctuations in sales growth and other sales patterns—seasonality, addition of new products, management changes, reduced competitive pressures, and so forth. For example, one of our largest clients, a leading provider of storage and data management solutions, has grown from $750 million in revenue to $1.5 billion in the four years we have been working with them. Whiteboarding is widespread there due to the important role whiteboard training plays in the organization's new-hire training program. However, it would be disingenuous of us to claim that whiteboarding is responsible for this growth. This is why we primarily rely on anecdotal feedback and repeat business rate as the best indicators of the success of whiteboarding as a better way to sell expensive stuff to educated buyers.

There are, however, examples of *independent* research that demonstrate the efficacy of using whiteboarding instead of PowerPoint slides. Surveys of 310 enterprise sales organizations conducted by Aberdeen Research (in conjunction with an October 2012 report titled *Train, Coach, Reinforce—Best Practices in Maximizing Sales Productivity*) found that:

1. 53 percent of Best-in-Class companies identified creating more meaningful sales conversations as a top priority to increasing/ sustaining revenue in an uncertain economy.
2. Conducting and leading an interactive whiteboard conversation (as opposed to a presentation or static slide deck) leads to...
   - 50 percent higher lead conversion rate
   - 29 percent shorter time-to-productivity (sales rep ramp-up)
   - 15 percent shorter average sales cycle
   - 2.5 percent higher annual revenue change year-over-year
   - 2.3 percent higher change in first year reps on quota

In addition to independent research, there are four primary ways we use to quantitatively measure overall whiteboarding initiative success. These are:

1. Post-training web surveys
2. CRM integration
3. Whiteboard certification
4. Controlled studies

Post-Training Web Surveys

A web-based survey three weeks after a whiteboard training session is one of the best ways to gauge the immediate results. It will tell you how the event was received, the initial impact on customer interactions, and in some cases the impact on average deal size when the whiteboard is used compared to the prior six months when it was not. We routinely run these surveys, and the data gathered tends to be very consistent. Here is a sampling of the questions we routinely ask, and the average responses calculated across dozens of surveys we have completed on behalf of our customers:

1. The whiteboard workshop increased your comfort level selling solutions and articulating your solution/product story.
   (a) Agree and strongly agree: 80 percent
   (b) Neutral: 14 percent
   (c) Disagree: 5 percent
   (d) Strongly disagree: 1 percent
2. Would you recommend this workshop/methodology to your peers or others?
   (a) Absolutely: 71 percent
   (b) Perhaps: 19 percent
   (c) No: 10 percent

3. Have/do you intend to use the whiteboard (or parts of it) in the field with customers and/or prospects?
   (a) I already presented it at least once: 41 percent
   (b) I presented it five or more times: 23 percent
   (c) I will present it soon: 36 percent

In some cases, it is possible to get quantitative results from sales data from these surveys. For example, in one survey we asked respondents to provide the deal size associated with specific sales opportunities when the whiteboard was used more than once, and found that on average it was 23 percent higher than the deal size calculated from CRM data dating back six months prior to the training. But as mentioned earlier, many other factors could have contributed to this increase.

CRM Integration

Another effective way to measure success is to ask sellers to identify when a whiteboard was used in conjunction with a particular sales opportunity, by checking a box or filling in a custom field in their CRM (Customer Relationship Management) system. There are a number of challenges with this approach, the least of which include training sellers on how to do this and why it is important. Another challenge is that the CRM system itself must be modified, which requires working through the IT or sales operations department, and perhaps waiting for the next release of the software before implementing the tracking mechanism.

However, in one case we were able to put this process in place, and the results were quite impressive. The data were gathered from more than 250 sellers, 1,000+ opportunities, and 600+ customers. Sellers used a drop-down field in their CRM system to indicate how the whiteboard was used, and data were tracked on total revenue but also on average deal size. The resulting data were impressive and reliable.

Whiteboard training was applied:	$280,000
Whiteboard training helped identify:	$225,000
Whiteboard training helped advance:	$335,000
Whiteboard training helped close:	$345,000

What this data unequivocally tells us is that the more sellers felt the whiteboard helped them, the larger the deal size. As the anecdotal feedback at the beginning of this section indicates, customers are indeed able to create their own buying vision when participating in a whiteboard dialogue, thereby increasing the overall opportunity size.

Certification

A surefire way to ensure that sellers who have been through a whiteboard training symposium know how to deliver the whiteboard "cold" is to get them into a room with an actual whiteboard and a panel of their peers or superiors. The exercise involves the seller going through the whiteboard presentation, "in role," during which the panel is working off a standardized score sheet and asking a set of questions or throwing out objections as the presentation progresses. Participants are measured not only on their knowledge of the whiteboard content, but also on a variety of other whiteboarding best practices (see Part 6). Once the data is gathered, it is tabulated and presented to sales management and other executives to demonstrate the level of uptake driven by the training event. The data can be sliced and diced by Area, Region, Team, and all the way down to the individual level. Ideally, each participant will receive a personalized report that documents their strength and growth areas, and how they compare to the other members of their team. While it doesn't measure impact on revenue, it is a good way to ensure some measure of ROI from the perspective of all the participants learning the material and increasing their knowledge ownership of the solution.

Controlled Studies

Probably the most effective (but logistically difficult) way to measure the efficacy of Whiteboard Selling's (or any methodology's) positive impact on sales metrics would be a controlled study of some sort, which, admittedly, we have never conducted. This study would involve putting half of a sales population through whiteboard training, leaving the other half out, and then tracking the sales performance of both groups over six months to a year. A study of this sort would require a statistically significant number of sellers, selling the same thing, in the same way, and controlling for a variety of outside influences that might impact one group over another. The reason we have never conducted such a study—aside from the logistical difficulties and room for error—is that sales and marketing leaders are frankly less interested in academic-minded studies with control groups and statistics, and more focused on enabling *all* of their sales resources to become more effective *now*, regardless of the approach (whiteboarding, negotiation skills, sales process, etc.). They've either witnessed the benefits of a sales training program firsthand, or heard about its impact through word of mouth from new hires or colleagues, and they don't need to see (or may not believe in) the results of a controlled study to tell them it works.

PART 6

You Have a Whiteboard, So How Do You Present It and What Do You Leave Behind?

CHAPTER 27

Whiteboard Presentation Best Practices

Regardless of whether you are an individual seller, a trainer, a marketer, or a sales executive, if you've made the investment to design and/or learn whiteboards for selling, a time will soon come when you will need to present it in a professional and competent fashion in a "live-fire" situation.

Rinse and Repeat

Even if you've been through a whiteboard symposium with the ability to present a whiteboard (or parts of it) to a customer or prospect the next day, you will still need ongoing practice to master all of the salient points and ensure you are 100 percent comfortable with the content and flow of the story. Here are seven steps that will enable you to master the visual content and story flow of *any* whiteboard in this book in two hours or less.

1. Grab a stack of plain white copy paper and a mechanical pencil.
2. For starters, just read through your whiteboard sales tool or other printout several times.
3. Now, put your sales tool aside, and following the whiteboard's step order, draw out as much of it as you can, beginning to end. *Do not look at your whiteboard guide!* You *will* miss stuff, but don't let that stop you—just keep going.
4. Review your whiteboard material and see what you missed.
5. Repeat steps 3 and 4 several times and you will have mastered the whiteboard visuals (the hard part).
6. Optional: Get yourself one of those four-color (red-green-black-blue) Bic ballpoint pens. Those just so happen to be the colors we use for our whiteboards. Once you have the visuals mastered with the pencil, try using the pen to get a feel for which colors are used where.
7. Now, layer in the script recitation on your next couple of go-arounds.

Once you have mastered the whiteboard on pen and paper, you can get together with some peers or, better yet, with a trusted customer, and present the whiteboard in role on an actual whiteboard, or over desktop sharing software using digital paper. It really doesn't matter to whom you present; it could be siblings, parents, friends, or even pets—one trainee actually presented to his dog because he was snowed in and couldn't get into the office to practice with co-workers!

Come Prepared

Make sure you have these three necessary tools at your disposal before you start whiteboarding.

1. Call ahead to ensure your meeting is scheduled in a conference room or office with a whiteboard.
2. Always bring your own set of dry erase markers in red, green, black, and blue, preferably the retractable type, so you'll avoid the problem of leaving the caps off your markers and drying out the ink.
3. Bring a package of "whiteboard wipes"—single-use towelettes that you can get at any office store. This will show your customer you have thought ahead, and it will give you just one more excuse to say, "I carry all of this with me because this is how I always present our story to our customers and prospects—we know you've seen enough PowerPoint!" You'll start the meeting off on the right foot when your customer smiles and nods in agreement.

Watch Your Stance

A very minor adjustment in stance can make a big difference when delivering a whiteboard presentation. Position yourself so your feet are perpendicular to the whiteboard surface, and be conscious to never alter this position except to turn and face your audience completely. It's a small detail, but it will prevent you from ever having your back to your audience. This rule doesn't apply very well to left-handed whiteboarders, but the principle still applies.

The *Lose-Your-Foot* Rule

A good way to remember that you must maintain a good stance is to imagine a laser beam or other limb-threatening device extends from the ceiling down along the x-axis of your drawing surface. If you ever move your right foot across this invisible line, then you'll lose a shoe size or two.

Engage

Because you are now using the open stance, you can truly engage your prospect in an interactive dialogue. Smile. Make eye contact. Use hand gestures. When whiteboarding in front of larger groups, remember to project and speak up a bit. This will help keep your audience focused on you instead of on their smartphones and tablets.

Avoid Dead Air

One of the most common missteps is to write on the whiteboard in silence, and then turn to your audience and regurgitate what you have just drawn, word-for-word. This creates an awkward pause that interrupts the flow of your presentation, giving your audience an opening to tune out and check e-mail. With just a little bit of practice—and by using the open stance—you can easily overcome this. Be sure to talk as you draw, then turn and face your audience to expand on the topic.

Slow Down!

If you are one of those sales professionals who wouldn't dare approach the whiteboard because you think you have poor penmanship, be prepared to surprise yourself. Bad penmanship is primarily a result of going too fast and not knowing your story. A good story is not a rushed story, so pace yourself, have fun, take time to engage your audience, and don't feel the need to scribble furiously on the whiteboard. The best outcome is when your prospect or customer writes "save" on the whiteboard, at which point it becomes an internal sales tool that lives on long after you have departed.

Manage Your Time!

A frequent question is, "How long should my whiteboard presentation be?" Naturally, this depends on the situation, the type of whiteboard, your audience, and their level in the organization. A general rule of thumb is that your basic solution whiteboard story should be 7 to 15 minutes long, if you were to present it without interruption. Once you add interaction, you could easily fill an hour-long time slot. In fact, because the whiteboarding approach is so engaging, you will frequently find that meetings start to run over, without objection from your prospects.

Based on how much time you have and to whom you are presenting, you can put in or pull out content as appropriate, and customize the basic whiteboard story flow. What is important is that you use the same basic content, visual structure, and flow, regardless of your audience. It would be impractical to have a different story line for each title in your target organization.

Go Virtual!

Using simple web conferencing software, and a revolutionary digital paper solution called *Papershow*, you can easily simulate a fully virtual whiteboarding experience at an extremely affordable price (about $175). This can make a big difference to your return-on-sales; you won't need to travel but you can still conduct a fully interactive sales call remotely through any standard web conferencing system. This approach does more than just save travel costs; you'll command greater attention from your prospects. We have found that while 50 percent of web conferencing viewers intermittently leave a remotely shared PowerPoint presentation to access e-mail and other applications, the attrition rate is less than 10 percent using the visual storytelling approach with digital paper.

Another benefit of digital paper over remote slide sharing is you can annotate the whiteboard with the feedback and input of your prospect (using a different color, perhaps), and then automatically create a PDF file of the whiteboard that you can e-mail directly to your prospect from within the *Papershow* application.

Dialing for Whiteboards

Whereas field personnel have the luxury of face-to-face interactions with prospects (either in a conference room or at lunch on butcher paper), inside salespeople should also have access to these techniques and a mechanism to engage and nurture leads early in the sales process, thus increasing conversion rates and shortening the sales cycle. If you are part of an inside sales team, just because you are not face-to-face with your prospect, it doesn't mean you cannot benefit from visual storytelling techniques. The virtual whiteboarding scenario described above allows you to have interactive dialogues and qualification discussions using remote whiteboarding. Imagine the difference between saying "I will send you an e-mail with more information" and "Do you have access to a web browser right now? Why don't we jump on a quick web conference so I can spend 10 minutes to show you what I'm talking about with a virtual whiteboard?" In this case you would use the *Papershow* digital paper discussed earlier, or another tablet-based drawing technology.

Whiteboards for Lunch

One of the most effective ways to use your whiteboard is at lunch with a customer on butcher paper at your favorite steakhouse, seafood joint, or pasta place, or after work for drinks at the bar on a paper placemat. Lunch at a restaurant is a neutral setting for an engaging interaction that is less formal than an office during business hours. The obvious time to pull out the pen is after you've ordered and before the food arrives. The conversation can continue over lunch and then wrap up over coffee, with documentation of concrete next steps. At the conclusion of your meeting, rip off the square of paper containing your visual discussion, fold it up, and hand it to your prospect or customer.

What kind of pen should you use? Pulling out a bunch of multicolored markers or crayons won't make a very good impression. Just bring along your handy Bic 4-color ballpoint. And one for your customer, of course!

Conclusion

Whiteboard Selling as a way to clarify your story using visuals is really a part of an overall sales transformation initiative. It is about aligning your sales force with the right message, the right customers, and the right solutions in a thoughtful and integrated fashion. It is not simply a matter of saying, "here's what to say and what to draw." It's all about getting salespeople and other customer-facing personnel to a point where they can deeply connect with a new value proposition and message, and then communicate that with nothing more required than a whiteboard or even a pad of paper. This is a critical component of elevating a sales team and delivering differentiated value to clients, prospects, and partners.

—Steve Rowland, Vice President, WW Sales

In *Whiteboard Selling—Enabling Sales Through Visuals*—we have endeavored to provide the reader with the background, tools, best practices, and an overall plan to build effective whiteboards for sales. We have observed these approaches working time and time again for organizations large and small to increase sales effectiveness and promote knowledge sharing and team building. But as Steve Rowland points out above, it is not just a matter of building whiteboards. It's about the role whiteboard selling plays in a strategic sales transformation program.

A Path Forward

So what now? Where should you begin? You probably have begun to some extent, based on our guidance throughout the book. Nevertheless, we've put together a worksheet of sorts that we hope will get you started down the right path toward putting some of the whiteboard concepts you have hopefully started into production. Of all the whiteboards you have prototyped or read about in this book, which is of the highest priority (see Chapter 8)? Fill out the following fields to get started on your first whiteboard initiative.

ACTIVITY

Whiteboard Type:
Whiteboard Objective:
Compelling Event (kickoff, regional training, other deadline):
Whiteboard Name:
Whiteboard Audience:
Whiteboard Deliverers:
Working Team Members:
Whiteboard Reviewers (partners, customers, analysts):
Enablement Models:
Other Whiteboard Uses (marketing, lead gen, etc.):

We wish you happy whiteboarding!

About Corporate Visions, Inc.

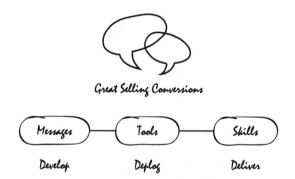

Great Selling Conversions

| Messages | — | Tools | — | Skills |

Develop   Deploy   Deliver

In B2B selling, it's ultimately the conversations that your salespeople have with prospects that have the greatest impact on decisions. Salespeople, with their lips moving, are your last bastions of differentiation.

So how do you create great selling conversations?

- **Develop provocative and differentiated messages** to clearly communicate why your prospects should change from their status quo, and change with you.
- **Deploy those messages** to the field in remarkable, field-ready sales tools and demand generation campaign content.
- **Train your salespeople with conversation skills** to deliver your message in a compelling way using the techniques described in this book.

This unique approach has been proven to work at companies such as ADP, CenturyLink, GE, Philips, Motorola, and many others.

Corporate Visions also provides automated software tools and technologies to support whiteboard design, development, and enablement, as well as consulting services to design whiteboards and run whiteboard symposium enablement sessions.

To see examples, get tips on messaging, and experience how customer-focused conversations can work for you, visit www.corporate visions.com.

INDEX